Richard Jones

The Growth of the Idylls of the King

Richard Jones

The Growth of the Idylls of the King

ISBN/EAN: 9783743408494

Manufactured in Europe, USA, Canada, Australia, Japa

Cover: Foto ©Thomas Meinert / pixelio.de

Manufactured and distributed by brebook publishing software (www.brebook.com)

Richard Jones

The Growth of the Idylls of the King

PREFACE.

WHEN our poet, holding in his hand a flower plucked from the crannied wall, cries, if he could understand it "root and all" he would then know what God and man is, he is affirming poetically that the process and the law of the mystery of growth is the key to the secret of the universe. He said well, therefore, who said that only when we understand the conditions under which a truth or a poem arose, or a political or philosophical system came to be, do we in reality understand what that is which has come to be. Or, as Professor Kuno Fischer has said, "To understand this poem ['Faust'] we must first of all understand its origin."

The subject-matter of the "Idylls of the King" grew and the poem itself grew,—the subject-matter during many hundred years, the poem during a half-century. This volume is a discussion of the growth of Lord Tennyson's version of the Arthur legend,—a version which may prove to be the classic English version of poetic material which has entered so largely into the literature of all European nations.

The effect of reflection upon the extent of this poetic material, these wide-spread legends, this stream of international poetry, is a disregard of the criticism that Lord Tennyson's ideal knight and blameless king is not the Arthur whom we know through Malory. In chapter i., section 4, there is an attempt to show that Tennyson's obligations to Malory have been overestimated, especially in the case of his Vivien, who can hardly be derived from Malory's lady of the lake, Nimue. The basis of chapter ii. is some early proof-sheets in the South Kensington Museum, and a printed copy, believed to be the only copy in existence, in the British Museum. The variations in these early texts, including also the MS. revisions not adopted, have a value to those who would therefrom discover the method of workmanship of this master of English metre, who is ranked in this respect among the greatest of English poets. In chapter iii. there is demonstration that the plan of the poem grew as the poet wrought. Finally, by determining the date of the various parts of the poem, we learn the poet's final view of life as expressed in this poem, and understand now why, notwithstanding the lines (written in early manhood) celebrating the power of prayer, the "Idylls of the King" closes with the darkness of that battle in the west where all of high and holy dies away.

I desire to express my obligations for many favors to Professors Rhys and Napier of the University of Oxford, to Professor Bülbring of the University of Groningen, and to Dr. Garnett of the British Museum.

RICHARD JONES.

SWARTHMORE COLLEGE, December, 1894.

CONTENTS.

CHAPTER I.
THE SUBJECT-MATTER OF THE IDYLLS OF THE KING.

	PAGE
1. A Similarity to Goethe's "Faust"	9
2. The Methods of Exposition applied to Goethe's "Faust"	14
3. The Arthur Legend, its Development and Dissemination	20
4. The Necessity for finding Tennyson's Sources, and the Method	28
5. Tennyson's Use of his Sources, and Comparisons with other Treatments by other Poets	42

CHAPTER II.
THE BEGINNINGS OF THE IDYLLS OF THE KING.

1. A Description of the Early Copies	44
2. The Variations in the Early Texts	50
3. Manuscript Revisions not adopted	58
4. A Summary of Variations in the Text	60
5. A Discussion of the Variations in the Text	100

CHAPTER III.
THE COMPLETED IDYLLS OF THE KING.

1. The "Idylls of the King" as an Organic Unity	113
2. A List of Variations between the First Editions and the Last Edition of the "Idylls of the King"	115

	PAGE
3. The Growth in the Plan of the Poem as indicated by the Changes made in the Language	133
4. The Growth in the Plan of the Poem as indicated by the Changes made in Consequence of the Introduction of the Allegory	140
5. The Philological Study of the Poetry of Tennyson	147

APPENDIX.

1. A Hitherto Unpublished Version of Tennyson's "To the Queen"	152
2. Tennyson's Punctuation and Use of Capital Letters	155
3. Is there another '57 Copy in Existence?	159

THE GROWTH OF THE IDYLLS OF THE KING

CHAPTER I.

THE SUBJECT-MATTER OF THE IDYLLS OF THE KING.

1. A Similarity to Goethe's "Faust."

THE "Idylls of the King," the noblest creation of Lord Tennyson's genius and the foundation of his highest fame, has been pronounced to be, not only this illustrious poet's greatest achievement, but also, indeed, one of the greatest poetical creations of the century. Of the first series of this poem Gladstone wrote in 1859 that the chastity and moral elevation of this volume, perhaps unmatched throughout the circle of English literature in conjunction with an equal power, recall the celestial strain of Dante. "Let those," he continued in glowing words, "who fear that the age of poetry is past, study this volume. Of it we will say without fear, what we would not dare to say of any other recent work, that of itself it raises the character and the hopes of the age and the country which have produced it, and that its author, by his own single strength, has made a sensible addition to the permanent wealth of mankind."*

To perceive more clearly exactly what this sensible addition is which Lord Tennyson has made to the permanent wealth of mankind, one may, doubtless, study to advantage the "Idylls of the King" in relation to its sources and the manner of the poet's use of these sources, in the same way as Goethe's "Faust" has been studied, with rich results, with reference to its origin and its composition as well as with reference to its fundamental idea. For Tennyson did not invent the subject-matter of the "Idylls of the King,"—viz., the mass of legend of various origin centering finally about the person of the Celtic hero, King Arthur,—these ideals of the centuries which he has woven together and, to some extent, transformed in retelling,—as Goethe did not invent the Faust legend which lies at the basis of his world-poem, or Homer the semi-legendary, semi-historical tales, which were given their final setting in those

> records of heroic deeds
> Of demi-gods and mighty chiefs,

the "Iliad" and the "Odyssey."

And, therefore, the methods of interpretation

* *The Quarterly Review*, London, October, 1859.

and exposition which have already been applied to Goethe's "Faust" may properly be applied also to Lord Tennyson's "Idylls of the King," as this likewise is a poem the subject-matter of which is largely the product of the imagination, not of the poet, but of the people, indeed, of many peoples widely separated in space and in time. The method of treatment would, manifestly, differ in the case of a poem struck off by the poet himself in a glow of inspiration, and in the case of a poem through which thus speaks the voice of the race.* In the interpretation of a poem like Goethe's "Faust" or Tennyson's "Idylls of the King" there would properly be large emphasis placed upon this contribution of the race to the poem.

Kuno Fischer, professor of philosophy in the Uni-

---

* Referring to the development of national poetry, Ten Brink says, " But herein lies the essential difference between that age and our own : the result of poetical activity was not the property and not the production of a single person, but *of the community*. The work of the individual singer endured only as long as its delivery lasted. He gained personal distinction only as a virtuoso. The permanent elements of what he presented, the material, the ideas, even the style and metre, already existed. The work of the singer was only a ripple in *the stream of national poetry*. Who can say how much the individual contributed to it, or where in his poetical recitation memory ceased and creative impulse began ! In any case the work of the individual lived on only as the ideal possession of the aggregate body of the people, and it soon lost the stamp of originality."—Ten Brink, " History of English Literature," p. 13. Henry Holt & Co., New York, 1889.

versity of Heidelberg, in his famed lectures on Goethe's "Faust" upholds the principle that *Dichterstoff*, the material of poetry, cannot be manufactured to order, averring that the interest of man is short-lived in that which has not already lived long in his imagination, that which he has not inherited, experienced, enjoyed, or endured. "Genuine poetic material is handed down in the imagination of man from generation to generation, changing its spirit according to the spirit of each age, and reaching its full development when in the course of time the favorable conditions coincide." He then emphasizes Goethe's good fortune in lighting upon a national legend, which was, as he was writing, still eagerly rehearsed at the fireside circle; and whose subject-matter was of national religious interest, because Dr. Faustus, who sold his soul to the Devil, was in the minds of the people in every way the antitype to Dr. Luther, who resisted the Devil and threw his inkstand at him in the castle of the Wartburg. This incident occurred in the same year in which, according to the legend, Dr. Faustus bargained away his soul for a career of pleasure in this world. Or rather, the date of the events in the great reformer's life determines the dates assigned in the legend to the wicked career of the great magician, who was to the people in every way anti-Lutheran, and whose career was, therefore, in their rehearsal of the facts of his life, made to contrast with that of Dr. Luther, the national hero.

So great was the popular interest in the Faust legends and so attractive, therefore, was the theme

THE SUBJECT-MATTER OF THE IDYLLS. 15

These methods of exposition, as they have been actually applied to Goethe's poem, are, according to Kuno Fischer,* 1st, the philosophical or allegorical; 2d, the historical; 3d, the philological. The kernel of all Faust literature is a religious fable of a nobly-striving and highly-gifted man, who, impelled by a thirst for truth and yet entangled by the pleasures of the world, becomes false to the service of God, strives after the power of magic, calls up the Devil and subscribes to him his soul for all eternity after he has enjoyed a wanton career in this life. This fable contains, even in its rudest form, momentous thoughts concerning the struggle between good and evil in the heart of man, concerning the motives which lead men to guilt and destruction,—clearly some of the profoundest themes of both religion and philosophy. Therefore Goethe's "Faust" is, by virtue of its origin, a religious and philosophical poem, which cannot be thoroughly comprehended without a knowledge of the ideas contained therein. The meaning of the poem was and is, therefore, a *philosophical* problem. The first attempts at interpretation took this direction. The problem was to explain the fable in "Faust,"—*i.e.*, to find the moral. This fable and its moral were taken to be allegorically portrayed in the persons and events of the poem. So the philosophical interpretation became allegorical interpretation, and this was followed

---

* This in regard to the "Faust" is substantially as given in Professor Fischer's university lectures.

by arbitrary interpretations, which soon ran into absurdities.

The entire poem seemed at last to be a sort of phantasmagoria, a world of enchantment wherein one could no longer trust his senses, but must look for a hidden meaning in that which appeared to be the simplest statement of a fact. A subtle meaning was given to the pedestrians before the gate, to the dance of the peasants under the linden-tree, to the revellers in Auerbach's cellar, to the wine which flowed from the table-top, the jewel-casket in Margaret's chest, the bunch of keys and the lamp with which Faust entered Margaret's prison-cell. It was even asked, what is the meaning of Margaret?

A substantially similar process of interpretation is already begun in the case of the "Idylls of the King." Not only is Arthur the King allegorized into a mere type of the Conscience, hardly in any sense a flesh and blood reality, but even Guinevere is taken to be no more the sinning queen, but a representation* of

---

* " It is said that Tennyson intended her, in his allegory, to image forth the Heart (or what we mean by that term) in human nature."—Stopford A. Brooke, "Tennyson," p. 357. G. P. Putnam's Sons, London, 1894. But Stopford Brooke's own view is that " she is a living woman, not an abstraction."

Van Dyke, referring to this tendency to interpret the poem as a strict allegory, says, "Suppose you say that Arthur is the Conscience, and Guinevere is the Flesh, and Merlin is the Intellect; then pray what is Lancelot, and what is Geraint, and what is Vivien? What business has the Conscience to fall in love with the Flesh? What attraction has Vivien for

the sensuous in man, and all the characters of the poem are taken to be types of some cardinal virtue or deadly sin, as in Spenser's gorgeous allegory, "The Faerie Queene."

To one of the early interpreters of the "Faust" the whole prison scene was symbolical of the Christian doctrine of belief. The bunch of keys with which Faust comes to free Margaret from prison was said to be a symbol of self-help, and the night-lamp betokened the shallow enlightenment of the understanding. The wine drawn from the table-top in Auerbach's cellar reminded one keen interpreter of the metamorphosis of plants, and the revelling students were in the opinion of another an allusion to the unbridled imaginations of the second Silesian school of poets!

But it was soon shown by the expositors who adopted historical methods that the fable was not invented by Goethe to suit the allegory, but was al-

---

the Intellect without any passions ? If Merlin is not a man, ' Que diable allait-il faire dans cette galère ?' The whole affair becomes absurd, unreal, incomprehensible, uninteresting."— "The Poetry of Tennyson," p. 176. Charles Scribner's Sons, New York, 1893.

For a valuable discussion of the allegory in the "Idylls of the King" see Elsdale's "Studies in the Idylls," Henry S. King, London, 1878, and the article by the Dean of Canterbury, one of Tennyson's university friends, in *The Contemporary Review*, London, January, 1870. The writer is, presumably, giving the poet's own interpretation of his poem, as he says, "This exposition, which is not, we beg to say, a mere invention of our own," etc.

ready in the older Faust compositions. The scene in Auerbach's cellar, which had been thus absurdly allegorized, was shown to have been substantially in some versions of the Faust legend, and so of other incidents in the poem.

Then began an attempt to find the origin of the "Faust" of Goethe in previous Faust compositions, an attempt carried by some to such an extreme as, in effect, to deny to the illustrious poet any power of imagination whatever.

Somewhat similar was the early criticism of Tennyson's poem, that he had borrowed outright from Sir Thomas Malory or Lady Charlotte Guest, merely putting into glorious verse the incidents of the old tales, adopting sometimes even the language as well as the story of the earlier versions,—a criticism which later was less often heard after it was seen that Tennyson was not merely retelling old tales, but was attempting to make a poem, an organic unity, out of the rich store of poetic material which had grown up about the chivalrous and spiritual ideals of the Middle Ages.

It is doubtless true, then, of Tennyson's "Idylls of the King," as of Goethe's "Faust," that to understand it fully we must understand its origin, that we may the better judge of the poet's thought in his poem when we know in what manner he has moulded and to what extent he has transformed the material wherewith he wrought. And though in this search for the poet's sources there may be a tendency to emphasize unduly the poet's obligations to his sources, nevertheless, only as we can trace the development of the ideal enshrined in the poem do we attain the critical rather than the dogmatic stand-point in our judgment of the poet's work.

The later problems of a philological or linguistic nature as to the time when the various portions of Goethe's "Faust," which was sixty years in coming into being, were written are much simplified in the case of the "Idylls of the King" by the fact that the members of the poem were published more immediately after their composition than was the case with the subdivisions of Goethe's poem, and we do not have the conflicts of opinion which have arisen as to the date of the composition of the various scenes of the "Faust,"—a matter which is of large importance, bearing as it does upon the growth of the poet's mind and his final view of life. There are lines in the poem near together in place but wide apart as the poles in thought. It is of vital consequence that we know, as we read, at what period of the poet's lifetime the views of life therein expressed were written, that we do not confuse the boy-poet's immature boyhood thought with the corrected opinion, the chastened judgment of the silver-haired sage, with the world-poet's final view of life.

But although the art of distinguishing by means of philological or linguistic tests between the earlier and the later work of the poet is not so important in the "Idylls of the King" as in the "Faust," yet there is a valuable study in connection with the changes made in the "Idylls of the King" in successive editions of the poem, and the reasons therefor.

In the universities of Germany semester-long courses of lectures on the " Faust" are given from year to year, though it is now more than a century since the first portion of the poem was published. These are among the largely attended * courses in the universities. It would seem that the fundamental thought of this poem is not yet exhausted, and that the rising scholars of this home of learning find substance in expositions according to the methods outlined above.

3. The Arthur Legend, its Development and Dissemination.

As the interpretation of Goethe's " Faust" is preceded by a *résumé* of the history of the Faust legend prior to its appropriation by Goethe, so will

---

* At the University of Munich I saw a hundred university students, unable to find seats, remain standing during the lecture hour to hear Professor Moritz Carriere's introductory lecture in his course on " Faust," a course which had been given for many years.

At the University of Heidelberg some three hundred hearers (among them gray-haired college men) daily enter the lists for the two hundred and seventy-five available seats in the lecture-room where Professor Kuno Fischer's lectures on " Faust" are given. Day after day, even through the hot summer month of July, notwithstanding the certainty that a score or more must remain standing during the entire lecture period, the press of hearers continues with unabated enthusiasm.

THE SUBJECT-MATTER OF THE IDYLLS. 21

a discussion of Lord Tennyson's treatment of his theme in the "Idylls of the King" properly begin with a study of the Arthur legend. The reader, having then some conception of the nature and possibilities of the matter wherewith the poet wrought, may form a judgment more entitled to respect as to the nature of the "sensible addition," which, according to Gladstone, this poem is to "the permanent wealth of mankind."

A critical study of the poem, then, inevitably begins with the accounts of the Celtic hero whose memory has been transmitted to us transfigured by legend, who historically was probably the leader of the Celtic tribes of England in their struggles with the invading Saxon hordes. His victory at Mount Badon (about 516 A.D.), described by Sir Lancelot to the household at Astolat,—

> Dull days were those, till our good Arthur broke
> The pagan yet once more on Badon Hill.
> . . . . and on the mount
> Of Badon I myself beheld the King
> Charge at the head of all his Table Round,
> And all his legions crying Christ and him,
> And break them; . . . .
> . . in this heathen war the fire of God
> Fills him: I never saw his like: there lives
> No greater leader,—

this victory is mentioned by Gildas in the sixth century, who, however, does not speak of him by name. Nennius, writing perhaps in the ninth century, speaks of this victory as one of the twelve won by Arthur* over the Saxon hordes.

But the struggle with the Teutonic invaders, however bravely and desperately fought, was in vain. As the cause of the highly-gifted, imaginative Celt became more and more hopelessly crushed in conflict with the kinsmen of the conquerors of Rome, he found solace in song for the hard facts of life. He won in the fields of imagination the victories denied him on the field of battle, and he clustered these triumphs against the enemies of his race about the name and the person of the magnanimous Arthur. By the Norman conquest of England the heart of the Celtic world was profoundly stirred. Ancient memories awoke, and, yearning for the restoration of British greatness, men rehearsed the deeds of him who had been king, and of whom it was prophesied that he should be king hereafter.†

Geoffrey of Monmouth wrote about 1132–35 A.D. (Ten Brink) a history of Britain in Latin, a book which, whatever its faults as a history, was an epoch-making book, because, though it did not originate the Arthur legends, it yet made them radiant

---

* "Duodecimum fuit bellum in monte Badonis, in quo corruerunt in uno die nongenti sexaginta viri de uno impetu Arthur; et nemo prostravit eos nisi ipse solus, et in omnibus bellis victor exstitit."—Nennius, edited by San-Marte, p. 69. F. A. Röse, Berlin, 1844.

† "But many men say that there is written upon his tombe this verse: 'Hic jacet Arthurus, rex quondam, rexque futurus.' "—Malory, Book XXI., chapter vii.

THE SUBJECT-MATTER OF THE IDYLLS. 23

with poetic coloring,* and thus contributed toward making them that which they soon became, the common property of Europe.† Geoffrey's book, still characterized as a work of genius and of imagination, is the source of a stream of poetry that flows to our day.‡ It was forthwith translated into French by Wace, who added the story of the Round Table. Within a generation or two innumerable versions, into which had been woven the legend of the Holy Grail, appeared among the principal nations of Europe, two of the more prominent writers being Chrestien de Troyes in France, and in Germany Wolfram von Eschenbach with his "Parzival," later the theme of Wagner's greatest opera.

The relations of these versions to one another, the questions as to which are the older and which

---

* "But above all the figure of Arthur now stood forth in brilliant light, a chivalrous king and hero, endowed and guarded by supernatural powers, surrounded by brave warriors and a splendid court, a man of marvellous life and a tragic death."—Ten Brink, "History of English Literature," vol. i. p. 135. Henry Holt & Co., New York, 1889.

† ". . . the Arthurian romances have exercised an immense influence upon the literature, not only of England and France, but of all European nations."—Dr. Sommer, "Le Morte Darthur," vol. iii. p. 1. David Nutt, in the Strand, 1891.

‡ "The effect of the work was therefore tremendous. Geoffrey's influence grew through the entire course of the Middle Ages, and spreading in a thousand channels, reached far into modern times, down to Shakspere, nay to Tennyson."—Ten Brink, "History of English Literature," vol. i. p. 136. Henry Holt & Co., New York, 1889.

are copies, and of which versions they are copies, the land of their origin, and the significance of the early myth,* these problems, weighty in tracing the growth of mediæval ideals, are yet under investigation by the specialists. It appears that five great cycles of legend,—1, the Arthur, Guinevere, and Merlin cycle; 2, the Round Table cycle; 3, the Lancelot cycle; 4, the Holy Grail cycle; 5, the Tristan cycle,—at first developed independently, were later connected together about the mediæval hero, King Arthur.† Even to run through all the available versions of the related legends is the task of a lifetime.‡

It is apparent that the centuries before Chaucer, far from being barren of literature, were periods of rich poetical activity. Geoffrey's book was written somewhat before the middle of the twelfth century. By the close of the century the theme, enriched by the illuminations of many men of genius and transfigured by the introduction of the San Graal, the

---

* " Leaving aside for a while the man Arthur, and assuming the existence of a god of that name, let us see what could be made of him. Mythologically speaking he would probably have to be regarded as a Culture Hero."—J. Rhys, " Studies in the Arthurian Legend," p. 8.

† Encyclopædia Britannica. Sommer says (p. 3), " Besides the Merlin, which presents the national story of Arthur, and the spiritual story of the Holy Grail, the Arthurian cycle has incorporated two other branches, viz., the ' Lancelot' and the ' Tristan.' "

‡ Lectures of J. Schick, professor of English literature in the University of Heidelberg.

holy vessel which received at the Cross the blood of Christ, the symbol of the Divine Presence, was engrossing the imagination of Europe. How were these poems so rapidly disseminated before the in- invention of the printing-press and our modern triumphs over time and space? We know that copies of the poems in manuscript were carried from country to country, but the more important means of dissemination were doubtless the minstrels, who passed from court to court and land to land. In the oldest specimen of English poetry that has come down to us, whose hero is Widsith, the far-traveller, we read (in modern words):

"Thus roving, the glee-men wander through the lands of many men, as their fate wills; they let their needs be known, and utter words of thanks. They find ever, in the north or in the south, some one who understands song, is not niggardly with gifts, who will exalt his fame before his heroes, and show manhood until all things disappear, even light and life. He who works praise has under heaven high and steady fame." *

The entertainment of these minstrels was splendid, not merely because of the natural desire to be spoken well of at the next court, but because the songs of the poet-singer were a stimulus to the intellectual life of hearers not surfeited with book-learned lore. The minstrel, the bringer of tidings from the out- side world as well as a glimpse of the higher realm of thought, treated with high consideration during

---

* Ten Brink, p. 12.

his stay at court, a chain of gold hung about his neck at his departure, passed from land to land singing the songs which he had made or heard. In that age there was little thought of literary proprietorship.* The poem belonged to him who could recall it. Even the manuscript was often marked with the name of the copyist rather than with the name of the author, thus making confusion worse confounded for modern scholars attempting to discover the original singer of the song.

And as each minstrel felt free to adopt whatever poem he found or heard that pleased him, so he felt free also to modify the incidents thereof, guided only by his experience as to what pleased his hearers.

---

* See note on page 11 in regard to early poetry as the product of the community rather than of the individual poet. The statement above as to the absence of literary proprietorship, as well as the preceding statements as to the honor paid to the poet-singer, apply perhaps more invariably to the earlier history of the Arthur legend. There is here no intent to touch upon the controversy between Bishop Percy and J. Ritson. The period of national poetry was now drawing toward a close, but it was not yet closed. Alfred Nutt, speaking of Wolfram von Eschenbach, who wrote his "Parzival" about the time when the Niebelungenlied were given their present form, and when the Arthur legends were already the common property of Europe, says (in "Studies in the Legend of the Holy Grail," p. 248), "Compared with the unknown poets who gave their present shape to the Niebelungenlied or to the Chanson de Roland he is an individual writer, but he is far from deserving this epithet even in the sense that Chaucer deserves it."

Hence the countless variations in the treatment of the theme, and the value of the conclusions which may be drawn as to the moral sentiments of an age the quality of whose moral judgments is indicated by the prevailing tone of the songs which persisted because they pleased. Unconformable variations, which express the view of an individual rather than the view of the race, may have come down to us in an accidentally-preserved manuscript, but the songs which were sung by the poets of all lands give expression to the view of life of the age, and reveal the morals and the ideals of nations whose history in this respect may otherwise be lost to us. What some of these ideals were, and what the corresponding modern ideals are as revealed in the "Idylls of the King," of which one has said that "it stirs the heart of this generation, and will not cease to do so until the ethical ideals and the philosophy of life which this poem enshrines shall, if that be their destiny, have wholly passed away,"*—this is a theme worthy of the philosopher and the historian, of the finished scholar able to interpret sympathetically the aspirations of each age and to trace the evolution of the ideals of the past into the realities of the present.

Surely, one can hardly overestimate the extent and importance of poetic material which has exercised so large an influence upon the literature of all European nations, nor ignore the nature and the possi-

---

* H. D. Traill, *The Nineteenth Century*, December, 1892.

bilities of this material when forming a judgment as to whether or no the "Idylls of the King" is the adequate treatment and the final form of this rich store of *Dichterstoff*, of poetic material handed down in the imagination of man from generation to generation through the centuries.

4. The Necessity for finding Tennyson's Sources, and the Method.

As a knowledge of the nature and possibilities of the subject-matter, this raw material of great poetry, is thus necessary for an informed judgment as to whether or no the "Idylls of the King" is the adequate and final treatment of this subject-matter, this stream of national, nay, of international poetry, so it is also necessary, in discussing more in detail the influence of particular sources upon the poet's treatment of his theme, to know which of the many available versions of the legend were in reality the sources drawn upon. For while the poet cannot treat legendary matter capriciously, yet there is large variety of treatment in the legends themselves, and therefore some criticisms which have been passed upon Lord Tennyson's ideal king, that "this is not the Arthur whom we knew"* (through Malory), may perhaps be based upon an overestimate of Malory as representing Arthurian legend or of Tennyson's obligations to Malory as a source. Malory's book, "incomparable" though it be in some respects,

---

* Andrew Lang in Sommer's "Malory."

THE SUBJECT-MATTER OF THE IDYLLS. 29

is yet a compilation, and not always a happy one, since, the delineations of the chief characters being taken from versions which developed differently, there are attributed to a single individual radically incompatible traits. There are, in reality, two Arthurs in Malory.* Furthermore, Malory sometimes follows a poor version of a legend, and is not thus in every case happy in showing the spiritual significance of these vehicles of profoundest religious truth, in revealing the heart of the mystery of legends which were often instinct with high conceptions and noble ideals.†

---

* One of Malory's Arthurs commits incest, and then to save himself from the doom predicted orders all children born on May-day to be killed. The other Arthur is Malory's "noblest king and knight of the world." Andrew Lang, after referring to Malory's book as a "jumble," says (in Sommer's "Malory"), "It was well called ' La Morte d'Arthur,' for the ending atones for all, wins forgiveness for all, and, like the death of Roland, is more triumphant than a victory." Swinburne (in his "Miscellanies") speaks of "the romantic Arthur of the various volumes condensed by Mallory into his English compilation,—incoherent itself and incongruous in its earlier parts, but so nobly consistent, so profoundly harmonious in its close,"—

† Alfred Nutt's comment on Malory is, " Malory is a wonderful example of the power of style. He is a most unintelligent compiler. He frequently chooses out of many versions of the legend, the longest, most wearisome, and least beautiful; his own contributions to the story are beneath contempt as a rule. But his language is exactly what it ought to be, and his has remained in consequence the classic English version of the Arthur story."—Alfred Nutt, "Studies in the

It is properly, then, no reproach to Tennyson that his ideal king is not the Arthur whom we knew through Malory, as he chose sometimes to follow another source. Indeed, Tennyson's obligations to Malory may easily be unduly emphasized. Malory was not of necessity his source in every case in which there is similarity of incident, for these tales

---

Legend of the Holy Grail," p. 236. Publications of the Folk-Lore Society, No. xxiii., London, 1888.

Dr. Sommer, after "four years of arduous labor" on his monumental edition of Malory, might well be pardoned some favorable bias in his estimate of the work itself. And yet his critical faculty is too honest to praise unreservedly. In his concluding chapter we read, "We owe the worthy knight a deep debt of gratitude both for preserving the mediæval romances in a form which enabled them to remain an integral portion of English literature, and for rescuing from oblivion certain French versions of great value to the critical student. But truth demands that we should not rate him too highly. To put it mildly, his work is very unequal—sometimes he excels, but often he falls beneath, oftener still, he servilely reproduces his originals. Nor can his selection of material be unreservedly praised. Difficulties in procuring MSS. may possibly have occurred of which we have nowadays no idea; yet, giving him the full benefit of this supposition, we must still say that he left out many of the most touching and admirable portions of the French romances, and that he has incorporated others of inferior quality. The most marked and distressing instance is his preference of the trivial and distasteful version of the Merlin and Viviene episode as found in the 'Suite de Merlin' to the exquisite version of the Vulgate-Merlin, which, in its mingling of wild romance and delicate sentiment, is perhaps the most beautiful and characteristic story of mediæval literature."

THE SUBJECT-MATTER OF THE IDYLLS. 31

were the common property of the poets of all lands. An outline of the story of Erec and Enid as told by Chrestien de Troyes in France in the twelfth century strikingly resembles the story of Geraint and Enid as told by Tennyson. Tennyson's source in this case was, as is well known, Lady Charlotte Guest's "Mabinogion." And yet there is far greater resemblance between Tennyson's "Geraint and Enid" and the twelfth century version than there is between Malory and some others of the Idylls commonly said to be drawn from Malory, or at least suggested by him.

As, for example, it is usually rather taken for granted that the source of Tennyson's "Vivien," in so far as it had a source, is Malory. Littledale's comment * is, "This Idyll . . . derives little more than a suggestion from the old romances. Malory simply tells how Merlin fell in a dotage about one of the damsels of the lake whose name was Nimue." Stopford A. Brooke refers to "the original tale in Malory." † Van Dyke, speaking of the changes of deep significance made by the poet, gives a selection from Malory and exclaims, "How bald and feeble is this narrative compared with the version which Tennyson has given!" ‡ Andrew Lang, comparing Malory with Homer, says, "In Nimue, one of the ladies of the lake, we have Malory's Circe, whose wiles are too

---

* "Essays on Tennyson's Idylls of the King," p. 170.
† "Tennyson, his Art and Relation to Modern Life," p. 306.
‡ "The Poetry of Tennyson," p. 150.

cunning even for his Odysseus. Merlin."* In the article on Geoffrey of Monmouth in the "Encyclopædia Britannica" we read, "And Tennyson's 'Idylls of the King' furnish the most illustrious example of Geoffrey's influence; although the poet takes his stories in the first instance from Malory's 'Morte Darthur,'" —a statement doubtless intended as a general statement admitting of important exceptions. Some four or five of the twelve Idylls owe little to Malory, one of these being, apparently, Tennyson's version of the Vivien episode.

There are, doubtless, suggestions from Malory in some incidents of Lord Tennyson's poem, "Merlin and Vivien," notably in the addition of six pages made to the poem in '74. But Tennyson's Vivien can hardly be derived from Malory's Nimue. It is true that Nimue makes use of a "charm," as does Vivien, but the motive for its use is altogether different. And in any case this use of a charm might have been suggested to Tennyson by other sources. This does not imply any obligation to Malory for the poet's conception of his Vivien, inasmuch as the Vivien of the "Idylls of the King" has in reality nothing in common with Malory's lady of the lake, "hight Nimue." Malory's Nimue is an entirely different character, altogether "more sinned against than sinning." Merlin was "assotted" on her through no wile of hers, and she worked the "charm" on him to protect herself and her virtue

---

* In Sommer's "Le Morte Darthur," vol. iii. p. xiv.

THE SUBJECT-MATTER OF THE IDYLLS. 33

from the power of his dreaded "enchauntments." Indeed, it would appear that the source of Tennyson's "lovely baleful star" cannot possibly be the lady of the lake of Sir Thomas Malory, as is evident from the following epitome, based upon the index of Sommer's "Morte Darthur," of every reference in Malory to the "damosell hight Nimue." *

---

* Dr. Sommer incorporates into his index references to the accounts of Nimue in Malory, but not every passing allusion to those accounts. Nor does he include under the name Nimue references to the lady of the lake who gave Arthur the sword Excalibur. She was a different character, whose head had been cut off by Balin long before Merlin became "assotted." But were every reference in Malory to any lady of the lake included under one figure, the conclusion must be the same, viz., that Malory's lady of the lake is not the prototype of the Vivien of the "Idylls of the King."

In connection with the question as to whether the various ladies of the lake in Malory were originally one or diverse characters, the following from Professor Rhys, of Oxford ("Studies in the Arthurian Legend," p. 348), is of interest: ". . . and considering how predicates, frankly inconsistent and contradictory, are applied to everything connected with the other world, there is no occasion to regard these two Morgens as forming distinct persons rather than one and the same fairy differently described. In a word, she is viewed at one time as kind and benevolent and at another as hostile and truculent. The same sort of remark applies to the same sort of person under the name of the Lady of the Lake, of whose figure Malory gives, so to say, widely different views. Accordingly, one Lady of the Lake sends Arthur the sword Excalibur and asks for Balyn's head in return for it; another Lady of the Lake confines Merlin in his stone prison; a

She first appears in Malory in Book III., chapter xiii., which tells how king Pellinore "gate the lady." She had been led away by force from, not Mark's court but Arthur's. Her kinsman had followed and "chalenged that lady of that knight, and said shee was his neere cosen." But while they were waging "battaile in that quarell" king Pellinore "anone rode betweene them," and announced that "the lady shall goe with me to king Arthur, or I shall die for it, for I have promised it unto him." He "clove downe the head" of one of them to the chin, and then "hee departed with the lady, and brought her to Camelot." There "Merlin fel in a dotage on the damosel that king Pellinore brought to the court with him, and she was one of the damosels of the lake which hight Nimue. But Merlin would let her have no rest, but alwayes he would be with her in every place. And ever she made Merlin good cheere, till she had learned of him all manner thing that shee desired; * and hee was so sore assotted upon her that

---

third, Nyneue, busies herself about Arthur's safety, and a fourth about that of Lancelot. They may all be taken as different aspects of the one mythic figure, the lake lady Morgen."

* The Nimue of Malory's compilation may perhaps not be consistent throughout. She who later in Malory is the trusted friend and adviser of both king and queen is here not quite sincere with Merlin. But surely the last charge which could be brought against her is that of harlotry. And her use of a charm to *protect* her virtue hardly makes her the prototype of Lord Tennyson's Circe, who plotted long fixt in her will to

he might not be from her. . . . And then soone after the lady and Merlin departed; and by the way as they went Merlin shewed her many wonders, and came into Cornewaile. And alwaies Merlin lay about the lady for to have her maidenhood, and she was ever passing wery of him, and faine would have beene delivered of him, for she was afraid of him, because he was a divels sonne, and she could not put him away by no meanes.

"And so upon a time it hapned that Merlin shewed to her in a roche where as was a great wonder, and wrought by enchauntment, which went under a stone. So by her subtile craft and working, she made Merlin to goe under that stone to let her wit of the mervailes there, but she wrought so there for him, that he came never out, for all the craft that he could doe. And so she departed, and left Merlin."

In chapter xvi. there is an account of "how the damosell of the lake saved king Arthur from a mantell which should have brent him," the bringer of the suspected mantell being by Nimue's "counsaile" compelled to put the mantell on, and "foorthwith" she was "brent to coles."

---

make the most famous man of all those times lost to use and name and fame.

The prototype of Malory's Nimue, the heroine of the "Suite de Merlin," was a high-born damsel, the daughter of a king, of great beauty and wisdom, who also preserves her honor. Unlovely as her character may be in some respects according to modern ideals, she is in no sense a Vivien.

The damosell of the lake next appears in chapter xxiii. of Book IV., where she brings Ettard into the presence of Pelleas, who was about to die on account of her rejection of his love. "And therewith she cast such an enchantment upon her that shee loved him out of measure, that well nigh shee was out of her mind. 'Oh, Lord Jesus,' said the lady Ettard, 'how is it befallen me that I now love him which I before most hated of all men living?' 'This is the rightwise judgment of God,' said the damosell of the lake. And then anon sir Pelleas awoke, and looked upon the lady Ettard. And when he saw her, he knew her, and then hee hated her more than any woman alive, and said, 'Goe thy way hence, thou traitresse, come no more in my sight.' And when she heard him say so, she wept, and made great sorow out of measure. . . . So the lady Ettard died for sorrow, and the damosell of the lake rejoyced sir Pelleas, and loved together during their lives."

She guarded his reputation by keeping him out of Lancelot's way, "for where as sir Lancelot was at any justs or turneyments, she would not suffer him to be there at that day, but if it were on sir Lancelot's side."

In Book XI., chapter xvi., she "that was alway friendly unto king Arthur, shee understood by her subtill crafts that king Arthur was like to be destroyed," and she again saves his life. In Book XVIII., chapter viii., she saves the queen's life.

And not only did she twice save the king's life, but she was also present at his death. "But thus was hee led away in a barge, wherein were three queenes; . . . and there was Nimue the chiefe lady of the lake, which had wedded sir Pelleas the good knight; and this lady had done much for king Arthur." The last reference to her in Malory is to the effect that "shee would never suffer sir Pelleas to bee in danger of his life, and so hee lived to the uttermost of his dayes with her in great rest."

Surely the Vivien of the "Idylls of the King" is not the Nimue of Sir Thomas Malory, since they have scarcely a trait in common. And though there are in the incidents of the poem suggestions from Malory, yet the character Vivien herself, so far as she is not Lord Tennyson's own invention, must evidently be sought for in other sources. And all criticism designed to illustrate the difference between the treatment of the subject by Tennyson and by Malory, based upon the supposition of Tennyson's obligations to Malory for his character Vivien, is labor lost.

In Lady Guest's "Mabinogion" there is a brief epitome of the account given in Southey's "Morte d'Arthur" of the incarceration of Merlin by the artifices of his Lady Love. The "fair Viviane" of this Romance resembles greatly the baleful siren of Lord Tennyson's Idyll. Though she at first "promised to be his true love upon honorable terms," yet to learn the charm, the "proof of trust" in Tennyson's poem, she "began to fawn and flatter him," and "for her great treason, and the better to delude and deceive him, she put her arms round his neck, and began to kiss him, saying, that he might well be hers seeing that she was his." When she had succeeded in obtaining the charm and had "put it all in writing," "then had the damsel full great joy, and showed him greater semblance of loving than she had ever before made." After he was asleep, "she made the enchantments," "and when he awoke, and looked round him, it seemed to him that he was enclosed in the strongest *tower* in the world." This expression reminds us of Tennyson's line describing the hollow oak in which Merlin lay as dead, "It look'd a *tower* of ruin'd masonwork." In Lady Guest we find also Tennyson's "wild woods of *Broceliande*" spoken of as the "forest of *Broceliande*" (in Malory's account "she and Merlin went over the sea unto the land of *Benwicke*"). The "fairy well" of the poet

> That laughs at iron—as our warriors did—
> Where children cast their pins and nails, and cry,
> "Laugh little well!"

is also mentioned in Lady Guest's book.

Inasmuch as the poet obtained the material for his "Enid" (1857)* from Lady Guest's "Mabinogion," it seems not improbable that the suggestion for his "Nimuë," published at the same time, may have come from Lady Guest also. At least his attention may have been directed to the romance itself by this epitome given in Lady Guest. Certain it

---

* See chapter ii.

is that the general character of the Vivien of the "Idylls of the King" bears a striking resemblance to "the fair Viviane" of Lady Guest's note, and bears no resemblance whatever to the Nimue of Sir Thomas Malory, who was the faithful wife of Sir Pelleas, and the trusted friend of King Arthur and his queen, both of whom she by her "counsaile" saved from death.

An excellent example of the laborious but fruitful study required for determining what the poet's sources really were is the monograph of Dr. Walther Wüllenweber, "Ueber Tennyson's Königsidylle, The Coming of Arthur."* He compares minutely Tennyson's introductory poem, "The Coming of Arthur," with some fourteen prior versions. He makes lists of incidents given in the poem and also in one or more of the other versions, and notes the agreements and disagreements in the details. Those versions in which the details agree with Tennyson are then compared as to still smaller details, as, for example, the spelling of the proper names. These lists of names in parallel columns, together with other lists of agreements and disagreements, point toward the poet's probable source. The following examples, taken from three of the fourteen versions under consideration, illustrate the agreements and disagreements in proper names. The first five names in the Tennyson column seem to have been suggested by Malory's "Morte Darthur;" the next

---

* Herrig's Archiv, vol. lxxxiii., 1889.

two, viz., Bellicent and Anguisant, were apparently taken from Ellis's "Specimens of Early English Metrical Romances;" and the last two, Gorlois and Igerne, suggest as Tennyson's immediate source the epoch-making volume, the fountain-head of Arthurian story, Geoffrey of Monmouth's "Historia Britonum." The names of Arthur's twelve battles, referred to in "The Coming of Arthur,"

> and in twelve great battles overcame
> The heathen hordes, and made a realm and reign'd,

and given in full in "Lancelot and Elaine," could have been taken only from Nennius,—unless, indeed, they were taken from some other version than the fourteen with which the comparison was made.

TENNYSON.	MALORY.	GEOFFREY.	ELLIS.
Leodogran of Cameliard.	Leodograunce of Camelyard.	(Incident is not given.)	Leodegan of Carmalide.
Ulfius.	Ulfius.	Ulfin.	Ulfin.
Brastias.	Brastias.	Bricel.	Bretel.
Bedivere.	Bedivere.	Bedver.	Bedwer.
Excalibur.	Excalibur.	Caliburn.	Escalibore.
Bellicent.	Margawse.	Anne.	Belicent.
Anguisant.	Agwisance.	Angusel.	Anguisant.
Gorlois.	Duke of Tintagil.	Gorlois.	Duke of Cornwall.
Igerne.	Igrayne.	Igerna.	

The result of these comparisons is the demonstration that Tennyson's "Coming of Arthur" agrees in minute particulars in some portion of the poem with Malory, with Geoffrey of Monmouth, with Ellis, and with Nennius. Whatever other sources may have influenced the poet, it seems probable that he was familiar with these four versions at least. The monograph seems to demonstrate that Ellis, whom the poet does not mention in the epilogue "To the Queen," influenced him (directly at least) more largely than Geoffrey, whom he does mention; and, more specifically, that it is Ellis who suggests Leodogran's query whether he shall give his daughter "saving to a king, *And a king's son*,"—an expression which was so skilfully employed by Tennyson in introducing into the poem, unavoidably apparently, an account of the birth of Arthur, the doubts as to his real right to the throne, the Barons' wars against him, whom they called baseborn, the founding of the Order of the Table Round, Merlin's vast wit, the Lady of the Lake symbolical of Religion, the brand Excalibur, the Sword of the Spirit. Indeed, substantially the whole of the "Coming of Arthur," which is the introduction to the "Idylls of the King," in which the persons and the events of the poem are sketched for the reader, arises naturally and seemingly inevitably out of Leodogran's uncertainty as to whether he should give his daughter "saving to a king, *And a king's son*,"—a suggestion which Tennyson seems to owe to Ellis.

It is true that the labor of ascertaining the sources which influenced the poet in the "Idylls of the King" would be enormous, and unjustified by the event, unless the poem be the adequate treatment of the rich store of Arthurian legend. But granting that the poem is worthy of exhaustive exposition, then the satisfactory answer to criticism such as Swinburne's, to the effect that Tennyson has given us an emasculated hero, no longer Malory's lusty, incestuous knight accustomed to "sweare prophane," but a creature far too good for human nature's daily food, or to Andrew Lang's regret that "this is not the Arthur whom we knew"* (through Malory), may be the demonstration that the obligations of Tennyson to Malory have been overestimated, and that, inasmuch as the traits of the ideal knight are to be found in the Arthur legend, Tennyson has done no violence to the spirit of the legend in its best estate in his portrayal of God's highest creature here, the highest and most human too, the blameless king, worthy to be also a type of the Conscience, of the higher soul of man.

5. Tennyson's Use of his Sources, and Comparisons with other Treatments by other Poets.

To discuss properly Tennyson's use of his sources, and to make a commensurate comparison of his treatment of the subject-matter with other treatments by other poets, would require a volume. And the volume has been written, Professor Maccallum's scholarly treatise, which gives to the "Idylls of the King," so far as one volume may, something of the treatment already accorded in Germany to the "Faust."

---

* This he said in the introduction to Sommer's "Malory." Had he been occupied at the moment, not with Malory but with other (and better) versions of the Arthur legend, he perhaps might not have greatly cared whether or no the Laureate's ideal knight and king be or be not the Arthur whom we know through Malory.

It may perhaps be true that only after such knowledge of the whole subject-matter as is implied in this treatment of Arthurian legend is one in reality entitled to express an opinion as to the rank to be finally assigned to Lord Tennyson's interpretation of this voice of the race. However this may be, a comparison of the treatments of the theme by various poets in various ages and in various lands makes more clear the real significance of the legend, enables one the better to grasp the heart of the mystery of this vehicle of profoundest truth.

To deny the necessity or the value of such exposition of the "Idylls of the King" as has been made of Goethe's "Faust," would be to deny in advance that the poem is a poem of the first rank composed out of elements which have been developed, not by the imagination of a single poet, but by the collective imagination of many peoples throughout many centuries of growth,—a denial which, if sustained, would doubtless be best sustained by showing, either that the subject-matter is not susceptible of such treatment as to produce a poem of the first rank,* or else that the poet's treatment of adequate material is in itself inadequate.

---

* "Thus the cycle of Arthur has not failed to enrich our modern poetry; . . . but a new epic it has not given us, because a new epic is an impossibility. Far hence, in the untravelled future, the echo of an age dimly heard, faintly understood, may become a song in the ears of men unborn. But we have not the epic spirit; ere that can come to birth, the world, too, must die and be born again."—A. Lang.

CHAPTER II.

THE BEGINNINGS OF THE IDYLLS OF THE KING.

1. A Description of the Early Copies.

In the preceding chapter, after a comparison of the "Idylls of the King" to Goethe's "Faust" and an account of the methods of exposition which have already been applied to the older poem, there was given a brief summary of the history of the Arthurian legend prior to its treatment by Tennyson. There now remains to describe the beginnings and the growth of the latest and greatest version of the old legend, the version characterized by Gladstone as in itself "a sensible addition to the permanent wealth of mankind."

Tennyson touched in early poems, such as "The Lady of Shalott," "Sir Galahad," "Sir Launcelot and Queen Guinevere," the legends connected with King Arthur of the Table Round, but the first published portion of the "Idylls of the King" was the noble fragment "Morte d'Arthur," which appeared in 1842, and in 1869 was incorporated into "The Passing of Arthur."

In 1857 there appeared a second portion of the "Idylls of the King," viz., six copies of two poems, which, after many changes, were republished in the first edition of the "Idylls of the King" in 1859, the name "Nimuë," however, being changed to "Vivien," another name for the character Nimuë found in some versions of the legends from which Lord Tennyson obtained the material for the poem. There is in the Library of the British Museum a single copy* of this book, which is believed to be "the sole survivor" of the "six trial-copies printed." † The title-page reads,

ENID AND NIMUË:

THE TRUE AND THE FALSE.

BY

ALFRED TENNYSON, D.C.L.,
POET LAUREATE.

LONDON:
EDWARD MOXON, DOVER STREET.
1857.

This sole surviving copy, "bearing Lord Tennyson's autograph inscription" † contains many tentative manuscript additions and corrections in the author's own hand. Exactly one-half of these corrections, leaving out of account changes in punctuation and other typographical corrections, were

---

* Presented to the Library by Mr. Francis Turner Palgrave, July 11, 1891.
† The catalogue of the Library of the British Museum.

adopted in the first edition* of the "Idylls of the King."

The corrections not adopted are of interest to us as showing the labor expended by the poet in attaining his acknowledged mastery of the art of expression, and as we may thereby learn something of his

---

* The growth of the "Idylls of the King" was as follows:

Morte d'Arthur	1842.
Enid and Nimuë (six copies)	1857.
The Idylls of the King	1859.
The Holy Grail, and other Poems	1869.
The Last Tournament	1871.
Gareth and Lynette, etc.	1872.
Balin and Balan	1885.

To the Table of Contents of the "Idylls of the King" as now published I hereby append the date of publication:

Idylls of the King,—
Dedication	1862.
The Coming of Arthur	1869.
The Round Table,—	
Gareth and Lynette	1872.
The Marriage of Geraint	1857.
Geraint and Enid	1857.
Balin and Balan	1885.
Merlin and Vivien	1857.
Lancelot and Elaine	1859.
The Holy Grail	1869.
Pelleas and Ettarre	1869.
The Last Tournament	1871.
Guinevere	1859.
The Passing of Arthur (Morte d'Arthur 1842)	1869.
To the Queen	1873.

literary art and follow him somewhat in the attainment of his preëminence as a master of style.

There is, however, a still earlier form of the poem "Enid" in the Forster Bequest Library of the South Kensington Museum. Here there is also a text of "Nimuë" like that of the British Museum copy, and a volume of late proof-sheets, the title-page of which reads,

THE

TRUE AND THE FALSE.

FOUR IDYLLS OF THE KING.

BY ALFRED TENNYSON,
P.L.; D.C.L.

LONDON:
EDWARD MOXON AND CO., DOVER STREET.
1859.

The four Idylls are "Enid," "Vivien," "Elaine," "Guinevere." The volume has been torn apart and the older forms mentioned above, viz., "Enid" and "Nimuë," have been inserted after "Enid" and "Vivien" respectively, and the whole has been rebound into one volume, the contents being "Enid" (the later form), "Enid" (the earliest form), "Vivien," "Nimuë," "Elaine," "Guinevere."

There are thus accessible for comparison with the text of the first edition of the "Idylls of the King" three older texts. These are,

1. "Enid" in the South Kensington Museum.
2. "Enid and Nimuë: The True and the False" in the British Museum. "Nimuë" in the South Kensington Museum.
3. "The True and the False. Four Idylls of the King" in the South Kensington Museum.

Of these texts the South Kensington "Enid" is the earliest print. Indeed, this may be the first "proof," as it contains some obvious compositors' errors, as, for example, "Droon" for "Devon" in the line, "I am Geraint of Devon," and "next" for "vext" in the line, "No, no," said Enid, vext, "I will not eat," and "lest" for "rest" in the line, "So moving without answer to her rest." It is not, however, the proof-sheet upon which Lord Tennyson indicated his revisions, as it shows but three manuscript corrections, while the differences between the South Kensington "Enid" and the British Museum "Enid" are many, as shown in the list of these differences following.

The pages in the South Kensington "Nimuë" and the British Museum "Nimuë" are numbered alike, and there is the same matter on each page. The British Museum "Nimuë" has but one manuscript correction. The South Kensington "Nimuë" is a "revise" upon which Lord Tennyson indicated many of the additions which were incorporated into "The True and the False. Four Idylls of the King" in 1859. The manuscript corrections to the South Kensington "Nimuë" which were not adopted are given in the summary of differences between the

THE BEGINNINGS OF THE IDYLLS. 49

various texts (page 89). Of more interest, however, than these manuscript corrections not adopted is the number of lines marked for omission and remarked "stet."

"The True and the False. Four Idylls of the King" (1859) does not differ materially from the first edition of the "Idylls of the King" published in the same year. There are, it is true, scores of minor variations. The "snake of gold" which slid from Vivien's hair shortly before Merlin yielded, when the dark wood was growing darker toward the storm, is in '59 a "twist of gold" round Vivien's head as she lay at all her length and kissed his feet. In "The True and the False" it was a "snake of gold" in both instances. The still earlier copies, however, the South Kensington and British Museum "Nimuës" agree in this case, not with "The True and the False," but with the "Idylls of the King." That is, we have in the first copies a "twist" of gold and a "snake" of gold; in "The True and the False," a "snake" of gold and a "snake" of gold; in the "Idylls of the King," a "twist" of gold and a "snake" of gold, as in the earlier copies.

The Table of Contents of "The True and the False" is Enid, Nimuë, Elaine, Guinevere. The name Nimuë is marked out with a pen, and a cross is placed before it; but the name Vivien is not written as a correction. In the poem itself, however, the name is given as Vivien throughout.

On the title-page of "The True and the False. Four Idylls of the King" the main title is "The

True and the False," which is in large type. Beneath, in small type, as a sub-title, is "Four Idylls of the King." However clearly the poet may have had in mind from the outset the plan of the whole as a single poem, the title grew from "Enid and Nimuë: The True and the False," to "The True and the False. Four Idylls of the King," and at last to the "Idylls of the King."

2. The Variations in the Early Texts.

The variations in these early texts, and the differences between these texts (including also the manuscript corrections not adopted) and the '59 edition, illustrate the pains taken by the poet in acquiring his exquisite command of the beauties of style.*

---

* "It may be doubted if any poet since the days of Horace and Virgil has been so great a master of the mere art of expression; . . . take him for all in all, he ranks the first of English poets in making the art of expression a luxury and an ornament."—*Edinburgh Review*, October, 1881.

"The music and the just and pure modulation of his verse carry us back not only to the fine ear of Shelley, but to Milton and to Shakespeare: and his power of fancy and of expression have produced passages which, if they are excelled by that one transcendent and ethereal poet of our nation whom we have last named, yet could have been produced by no other English minstrel."—Gladstone, *Quarterly Review*, London, October, 1859.

"The 'Idylls' may doubtless claim to be, in a technical sense, the poet's masterpiece. . . . Milton himself has not maintained so uniform a level of force and dignity or so seldom marred the flow of his numbers by a weak or ineffective line.

For though he had, indeed, "a gift of felicitous and musical expression which it would be no exaggeration to describe as marvellous,"* yet this gift did not preclude the necessity for an occasional gilding of the refined gold of his thought and the addition of another hue unto the rainbow of his expression.

In the oldest print of "Enid," the South Kensington "proof," after Earl Limours had

>moved the Prince
>To laughter and his *menay* to applause,

which in the British Museum copy is,

We cannot fairly compare the rhythms of the two poets at their best, for they are essentially different, but in the avoidance of monotony by the variation of cæsura and cadence, Milton is not the more successful and cunning of the two. And Tennyson's clear harp has been modulated to tones incomparably more diverse than ever rang from the Puritan's mighty lyre. He has attuned it to every voice of Nature, and its chords have resounded with the same resounding volume, the same unerring truth to every mood of man. The shock of spears, the sound of waters, the wailing of the winds —it answers to them all. It can trip as lightly as the sandalled foot of the maiden, and stride as starkly as the warrior's mail-clad heel. It can moan with the conscience-stricken Guinevere, or flash into wrath with the outraged Isolt, or swell into a strain of majestic melancholy with the dying king. In a word, the compass and capabilities of this simplest, yet most difficult, of English rhythms have never, since Shakespeare, been so magnificently displayed."—H. D. Traill, *Nineteenth Century*, London, December, 1892.

* Collins, "Illustrations of Tennyson," p. 177. Chatto & Windus, London, 1891.

>   moved the Prince
>   To laughter and his *comrades* to applause,

he obtains permission of Geraint to cross the room and speak

>   To your good damsel there who sits apart
>   And seems so lonely.

Having Geraint's free leave,

>   Then rose Limours and looking at his feet
>   Like one that tries *new* ice if it will bear,

a line which in the British Museum copy is,

>   Like one that tries *old* ice if it will bear,

and in the '59 edition,

>   Like *him who* tries *the bridge he fears may fail*,

he urges Enid to fly with him,

>   The one true lover *which* you ever *had*,

alleging that Geraint loves her no more. In the South Kensington text Earl Limours says to Enid,

>   your wretched dress,
>   A wretched insult on you, dumbly *shrieks*
>   Your story, that this man loves you no more.

But in the second text, instead of the exaggerated and impossible "dumbly shrieks" of the first text, we have,

>   your wretched dress,
>   A wretched insult on you, dumbly *speaks*
>   Your story, that this man loves you no more.

The discovery of an early text of the Faust, the Göchhausen copy, has made it manifest that Goethe also sometimes failed in finding at once the simplest and best expression. The less happy phraseology of the early text has later been corrected and ennobled. The Monologue of Margaret at the spinning-wheel, "this most perfect outburst of woman's love-longing," yet contains in its original form one passage wherein the poet overlooked the simplest and best and most obvious expression, and chose instead the coarsest and rudest. Instead of "My bosom yearns for him alone," we read in the early text, "Mein Schoos! Gott! drängt sich nach ihm hin." *

The differences between the early copies of these poems of the "Idylls of the King" are, however, often curious rather than important. There is a singular inversion of the order of the words in the two lines of the South Kensington "Enid" in which Geraint

> bared the column of his knotted throat,
> The massive heroic of his square breast.

In the British Museum copy Geraint

> bared the knotted column of his throat,
> The massive square of his heroic breast.

One line in the South Kensington "Enid" reads,

> Thy wheel and *thee* are shadows in the cloud.

---

* From Kuno Fischer, Die Erklärungsarten des Goetheschen Faust. Heidelberg, 1889.

In the South Kensington "Enid" we read,

> How many among *us* at this very hour
> Do forge a life-long trouble for *them*selves,

which later becomes, for *ourselves.*

Some lines of the South Kensington or the British Museum copy are omitted in the '59 edition, but more frequently new lines are added. The following three lines of the South Kensington "Enid" become seven lines in the British Museum copy, and eight lines broken by a paragraph in the '59 edition,

> K. Then call'd Geraint for wine and goodly cheer
> To feed the sudden guest, and Earl Limours
> Drank till he jested with all ease,
> B. M. Then call'd Geraint for wine and goodly cheer
> To feed the sudden guest, *and bad the host
> Call in what men soever were his friends,
> And feast with these in honour of their earl;
> ' And care not for the cost; the cost is mine.'
> And wine and food were brought,* and Earl Limours
> Drank till he jested with all ease,
> '59. Then cried Geraint for wine and goodly cheer
> To feed the sudden guest, *and sumptuously
> According to his fashion,* bad the host
> Call in what men soever were his friends,
> And feast with these in honour of their earl;
> ' And care not for the cost; the cost is mine.'
>
> And wine and food were brought, and Earl Limours
> Drank till he jested with all ease,

In these lines the latter form bears the closer resemblance to the account* in the source of the poem, viz., the "Mabinogion" of Lady Charlotte Guest, though in several cases the earlier text keeps closer to the original.

The following selection is exactly as printed in the oldest form of the poem, viz., the South Kensington "Enid":

'O, my new mother, be not wroth or grieved
At your new son, for my petition to her.
When late I left Caerleon, our great Queen,
In words whose echo lasts, they were so sweet,
Made promise that whatever bride I brought,
Herself would clothe her like the sun in Heaven.
Thereafter, when I reach'd this ruin'd hold
Beholding one so bright in dark estate,
I vow'd that could I gain her, our kind Queen,
No other hand but hers, should make your Enid burst
Sunlike from cloud—and likewise thought perhaps,
That service done so graciously would bind
The two together, for I wish the two
To love each other. Enid cannot find
A nobler friend: another thought I had,
I came among you here so suddenly,
I told my love for her so suddenly,
That tho' her gentle presence at the lists

---

* "And Geraint inquired of the man of the house, whether there were any of his companions that he wished to invite to him, and he said that there were. 'Bring them hither, and entertain them at my cost with the best thou canst buy in the town.' And the man of the house brought there those whom he chose, and feasted them at Geraint's expense."—The "Mabinogion," p. 169. London, 1877.

Might well have served for proof that I was loved,
I doubted whether filial softness in her,
Or waxen nature had not let itself
Be moulded by your wishes for her weal—
Or whether some false sense in her own self
Of my contrasting brightness, overbore
Her fancy dwelling in this dusky hall,
And that same sense might make her long for court
And all its dangerous glories; and I thought,
That could I someway prove that force in her
Linkt with such love for me, that at a word
(No reason given her) she could cast aside
A splendour dear to women, new to her
And therefore dearer, or if not so new
Yet therefore tenfold dearer by the power
Of intermitted custom, then I felt
That I could rest a rock in ebbs and flows,
Fixt on her faith : now therefore I do rest,
A prophet certain of my prophecy,
That never shadow of mistrust can cross
Between us. Grant me pardon for my thoughts,
I have not kept them long. I promise you
That when we come once more, as come we shall,
To see you, she shall wear your noble gift,
Here at your own warm hearth, with, on her knee,
Who knows? another gift of the high God,
Which maybe shall have learn'd to lisp you thanks.'
Then smiled the mother, pleased, but half in tears
To hear him talk so solemnly and well:
And brought a mantle down and wrapt her in it,
And claspt and kiss'd her, and they rode away.

In the last thirty-seven lines of the selection there
are ninety-seven variations from the text of the '92

edition. There were changes made in the selection in '57, '59, and '73. The "waxen" nature of the South Kensington "Enid," which Geraint feared had let itself be moulded by the wishes of parents, becomes her "easy" nature in the British Museum copy, " and that same" sense, which might make her long for court and all its dangerous glories, becomes "and such a" sense in '57, while the "dangerous" glories become "perilous" glories in '73.

In addition to the one hundred and three changes actually made in this selection, there are in the British Museum copy two manuscript revisions which were not adopted,—*knew* for *felt* in the lines,

> then I felt
> That I could rest a rock in ebbs and flows,

and the lines,

> Grant me pardon for my thoughts,
> I have not kept them long. I promise you
> That when we come once more, as come we shall,
> To see you, she shall wear your noble gift,

were so corrected that, if the manuscript corrections had been followed, they would have read,

> Grant me pardon for my thoughts,
> I have not kept them long. *I pledge my faith*
> *That Enid, when we come, some golden day,*
> *As come we will,* shall wear your noble gift,

This correction, however, was not the one adopted, and the lines appeared in '59 as,

58   IDYLLS OF THE KING.

>   Grant me pardon for my thoughts:
>   *And for my strange petition I will make
>   Amends hereafter by some gaudy-day,
>   When your fair child* shall wear your *costly* gift

and with this change there disappeared in '59 the '57 line, which made the mother "pleased"

>   To hear him talk so solemnly and well.

3. Manuscript Revisions not adopted.

There is a difference of opinion among lovers of Tennyson with regard to the value of the changes which the poet introduced into successive editions of his works. To some—unwilling, perhaps, to see the jewel of his thought, which was in a form already approved and familiar, given a new and strange setting—these successive refinements are occasionally but attempts to paint the lily and throw a perfume on the violet. Whether Lord Tennyson's literary taste was always unerring enough to restrain him from finally adopting tentative improvements which are no improvement is, perhaps, a matter of taste. But that he attempted improvements which did not finally commend themselves to his own taste is a matter of fact.

The first autograph correction, aside from punctuation, in the '57 (British Museum) copy is to the five lines,
>   and everywhere
>   Was hammer laid to hoof, and the hot hiss
>   And bustling whistle of the squire who scour'd
>   His master's armour; and of such a one

He ask'd, 'What means the tumult in the town?'
Who said, 'The sparrow-hawk, you ask that know.'

The words *Was hammer laid to* have been struck out and above them has been written *The clink of hammer'd*. The word *armour* is also crossed out and the word *arms* written above. The pen was drawn through the whole of the fourth line and above it was written, '*What means the noise & hurly burly here*'? The fifth, or last, line was also crossed out and above it was written, *Was answer'd O fair lord, the sparrow-hawk.*' None of these corrections were adopted. Yet the '59 edition differs from the '57 copy. In '59 we have, instead of *squire*, *youth*. The last line, which in the '57 copy reads,

Who said, 'The sparrow-hawk, you ask that know.'

is in '59,

Who told him, scouring still 'The sparrow-hawk!'

That is to say, after making the trial corrections on the '57 copy as quoted above, Lord Tennyson, adopting none of these, printed the first four lines in '59 as they were originally in the '57 copy (with the exception of one word), and revised again the fifth line, so that as printed in '59 it agrees neither with the '57 copy nor with the manuscript revisions thereof.

The manuscript corrections in the early texts which were not adopted in '59 are given in the summary of variations on the pages following. Our interest in these tentative, experimental forms of expression need not be an idle curiosity, for by means of these we are enabled to see to some extent the workings of the poet's mind. His version of the Vivien legend is a chaste presentation of a disagreeable subject. By a study of these early texts we learn with what care Lord Tennyson sought to avoid as far as possible the disagreeable features inherent in the subject. There are certain lines which were marked in the South Kensington "Nimuë" as though for omission and then re-marked "stet," doubtless as being indispensable to a description of the state of society produced by Vivien and her kind.

4. A Summary of Variations in the Text.

The poetry of Lord Tennyson furnishes an admirable basis for textual criticism because of the changes which occur in successive editions of the same poem. And inasmuch as Tennyson is a consummate artist, we may assume that these changes have not been due to mere caprice. To students of Tennyson, therefore, the following summary of variations * in the text may not prove unwelcome.

---

* With the courteous permission and kindly encouragement of Dr. Richard Garnett, Keeper of Printed Books in the British Museum, I collated " Enid and Nimuë : The True and the False" as printed in '57 with the poems as published in '59, noting also the changes in the successive editions of '62, '69, '73, '75, '84, '86, '90, and '92.

For the collation of the South Kensington copies I am in-

THE BEGINNINGS OF THE IDYLLS. 61

As to the changes made since '59 the summary is, in all probability, not exhaustive. The difficulty of making a *complete* list of variations in successive editions may be inferred from the publishers' note to the '93 edition of "The Works of Tennyson,"

Printed by R. & R. Clark, January 1884. Reprinted, with slight corrections, April 1884. Reprinted February and October 1885; May 1886; with slight alterations, December 1886. Reprinted 1887; May and November 1888; with many additions, February 1889. Reprinted April and December 1889; June and November 1890; July and December 1891. Complete edition with additions, January 1893. Reprinted May 1893.

It is difficult to procure copies of all these editions printed " with slight alterations," as even the Library of the British Museum does not contain a copy of every edition of the works of him who "ranks the first of English poets in making the art of expression a luxury and an ornament," * " one of the greatest masters of metre, both simple and sonorous, that the English language has ever known." †

In the following summary there are given the more important variations in the early texts, many mere typographical variations and variations in punctuation being not included. By K. is designated the South Kensington Museum " Enid," the first print

---

debted to Mr. D. Guernsey Jones of the University of Heidelberg.

* *Edinburgh Review*, October, 1881.
† *Macmillan's Magazine*, December, 1872.

of the poem; by '57, the British Museum "Enid and
Nimuë: The True and the False;" by MS., the manuscript revisions in this British Museum '57 copy
which were not adopted in '59; and by '59, the first
edition of the "Idylls of the King." References to
page and line are to page and line of the complete
edition of the "Idylls of the King," in one volume,
published by Macmillan & Co., London, 1889, and reprinted in '91, '92, '94. The first number within a
parenthesis following a quotation from the poem is
the number of the page upon which the quotation
may be found in the edition above cited, the second
number is the number of the line upon this page.
For example, the first line quoted (85, 4) is the
fourth line of the eighty-fifth page of the Macmillan
edition of the "Idylls of the King."

ENID.

'57. Had *wedded* Enid, Yniol's only child,
'69. Had *married* Enid, Yniol's only child, (85, 4.)

'57. And therefore, till the king himself should please
    To cleanse this common *shore* of all his realm,
'59. And therefore, till the king himself should please
    To cleanse this common *sewer* of all his realm, (86, 20.)

'57.   the *p*rince and Enid rode,
    And fifty knights rode with them, to the *ford*
    Of Severn,
'59.   the *P*rince and Enid rode,
    And fifty knights rode with them, to the *shores*
    Of Severn,   (86, 25.)

THE BEGINNINGS OF THE IDYLLS.

'57. At last, it chanced that on a summer morn
(They sleeping each by *other*) the new sun
Beat thro' the blindless *casements* of the room, (87, 24.)

In '59 *casements* is changed to *casement;* and in '69, *other* to *either.*

K. And bared the column of his *knotted* throat,
The massive *heroic* of his *square* breast,
'57. And bared the *knotted* column of his throat,
The massive *square* of his *heroic* breast, (88, 3.)

'57. At this he *snatch'd* his *great* limbs *from the* bed,
'59. At this he *hurl'd* his *huge* limbs *out of* bed,* (90, 1.)

'57.   And Enid *wonder'd at him:*
But *then* bethought her of a faded silk,
'59.   And Enid *ask'd, amazed,*
'*If Enid errs, let Enid learn her fault.*'
But he, '*I charge you, ask not but obey.*'
Then she bethought her of a faded silk, (90, 8.)

'57. But Guinevere lay late into the morn,
Lost in sweet dreams, and dreaming of her love
For *Launcelot,* and forgetful of the hunt; (91, 8.)

We have this spelling of *Launcelot,* which is the same as in Tennyson's early poem, "Sir Launcelot and Queen Guinevere," three times in the '57 copy,— as given above, and in the lines (86, 7),

But when a rumour rose about the Queen,
Touching her guilty love for *Launcelot,*

---

* See discussion of this line in Appendix.

and once in "Nimuë" (197, 13), just before Vivien's song in which occurs the reference to "the little rift within the lute That by and by will make the music mute." She says, "I heard the great Sir *Launcelot* sing it once."

'57.   and everywhere
Was hammer laid to hoof, and the hot hiss
And bustling whistle of the *squire* who scour'd
His master's armour; and of such a one
He ask'd, 'What means the tumult in the town?'
Who *said*, 'The sparrow-hawk, *you ask that know.*'

MS.   and everywhere
The clink of hammer'd hoof, and the hot hiss
And bustling whistle of the squire who scour'd
His master's *arms;* and *asking one of these*
'*What means the noise & hurly burly here*'?
Was answer'd O fair lord, the sparrow-hawk'

'59.   and everywhere
Was hammer laid to hoof, and the hot hiss
And bustling whistle of the *youth* who scour'd
His master's armour; and of such a one
He ask'd, 'What means the tumult in the town?'
Who *told him, scouring still* 'The sparrow-hawk!'
(95, 3.)

'57. *He* answer'd gruffly, 'Ugh! the sparrow-hawk.'
MS. *And had for answer,* 'Ugh! the sparrow-hawk.'
'59. *Who* answer'd gruffly, 'Ugh! the sparrow-hawk.'
(95, 13.)

'57. Then riding further past an armourer's,
MS. Then riding further past an armourer's *booth,*

'57. Sat riveting a *skull-cap* on his knee,
'59. Sat riveting a *helmet* on his knee, (95, 16.)

K. *At this* Geraint flash'd into sudden spleen :—
'A thousand pips eat up your sparrow-hawk
Who think the rustic cackle of your bourg
The murmur of the world! What is it to me?
A wretched set of sparrows, one and all,
Who pipe of nothing but of sparrow-hawks!
Speak, if you be not like the rest, hawk mad,
Where can I get me harbourage for the night?'

. . . .

And there is scantly time for half the work.
Lodging, in truth, good truth, I know not, save,
It may be, at Earl Yniol's, o'er the bridge
Yonder.' He spoke and fell to work again.

'57. *Whereat* Geraint flash'd into sudden spleen :
'A thousand pips eat up your sparrow-hawk *!*
Tits, wrens, and all wing'd nothings peck him dead!
You think the rustic cackle of your bourg
The murmur of the world! What is it to me?
O wretched set of sparrows, one and all,
Who pipe of nothing but of sparrow-hawks!
Speak, if you be not like the rest, hawk-mad,
Where can I get me harbourage for the night?
And arms, arms, arms to fight my enemy? Speak !'

. . . .

Arms? truth, I know not: all are wanted here.
Harbourage? truth, good truth, I know not, save,
It may be, at Earl Yniol's, o'er the bridge
Yonder.' He spoke and fell to work again. (95, 20.)

'57. Came forward with the helmet yet in hand (96, 7)
And answered, 'Pardon me, O stranger knight,
MS. Came forward with the *skull-cap* yet in hand
And O '*said he pardon me* stranger knight;
'59. Came forward with the helmet yet in hand
And answer'd, 'Pardon me, O stranger knight;

In the British Museum copy the word *helmet* (in the line 96, 7) is crossed out and *skull-cap* is written below. But this correction was not adopted. It is of interest in this connection that we find in the '57 copy, a few lines above, not *helmet* but *skull-cap*. The two lines are:

'57. Sat riveting a *skull-cap* on his knee. (95, 16.)
'57. Came forward with the *helmet* yet in hand. (96, 7.)

Apparently, in order to be consistent the poet changed the *helmet* in the latter line to *skull-cap*, the term applied in the line above. But later, ignoring this correction, he made the change in the first line, so that the '57 line,

Sat riveting a *skull-cap* on his knee,

in '59 reads,

Sat riveting a *helmet* on his knee.

In one other instance the '57 copy has *skull-cap*, which was changed to *helmet* in '59, the line (107, 16),

'57. And crackt the *skull-cap* thro', and bit the bone.

In the '57 copy Geraint once " aim'd at the " *helm*" of his enemy, and Earl Doorm " doff'd his *helm*." In the " Mabinogion," Geraint on two distinct occasions broke his enemy's " head-armour" and " wounded the bone."

K. But in, go in ; for save yourself desire it
We will not touch upon him ev'n in *game*.'

'57. But in, go in; for save yourself desire it
   We will not touch upon him ev'n in *jest*. (97, 6.)

K. Thy wheel and *thee* are shadows in the cloud;
'57. Thy wheel and *thou* are shadows in the cloud;
                                                (99, 5.)
'57. 'Hark, by the bird's song you may learn the nest'
   Said Yniol; 'Enter quickly.' Entering then
   The dusky-rafter'd, many-cobweb'd Hall,
'59. 'Hark, by the bird's song you may learn the nest'
   Said Yniol; 'Enter quickly.' Entering then,
   Right o'er a mount of newly-fallen stones,
   The dusky-rafter'd, many-cobweb'd Hall, (99, 8.)

'57. But none spake word except the hoary Earl:
   'Enid, the good knight's horse stands in the court;
   Take him to stall and give him *corn*, and *then*
   Go to the town and buy us flesh and wine;
   And we will make us merry as we may.
MS. But none spake word except the hoary Earl:
   Rest, friend: the maiden serves: it is her wont:
   'Enid, the good knight's horse stands in the court;
   Take him to stall and give him *food*, and *thence*
   Go to the town and buy us flesh and wine;
   And we will make us merry as we may.
'59. But none spake word except the hoary Earl:
   'Enid, the good knight's horse stands in the court;
   Take him to stall, and give him corn, and then
   Go to the town and buy us flesh and wine;
   And we will make us merry as we may. (99, 17.)

'57. Our hoard is little, but our hearts are great.'
      Then Enid took *the knight's horse* to the stall,
   And litter'd him and gave him hay and corn;
   And after went her way across the bridge,

'59. Our hoard is little, but our hearts are great.'
>   He spake: the Prince, as Enid past him, fain
>   To follow, strode a stride, but Yniol caught
>   His purple scarf, and held, and said ' Forbear !
>   Rest ! the good house, tho' ruin'd, O my Son,
>   Endures not that her guest should serve himself.'
>   And reverencing the custom of the house
>   Geraint, from utter courtesy, forebore.
>   So Enid took *his charger* to the stall ;
>   And after went her way across the bridge, (99, 22.)

The '57 line describing Enid's care of Geraint's horse, "And litter'd him and gave him hay and corn," omitted in '59, is in the " Mabinogion," "and then she furnished his horse with straw and with corn."

The reader in whose mind is fresh the admiring exclamation of the Prince,

>   Here, by God's grace, is the one voice for me,

and

>   Here by God's rood is the one maid for me,

can well approve the poet's rejection of the manuscript line written in the '57 copy, but not found in the '59 edition,

>   *Rest, friend: the maiden serves: it is her wont:*

a line which lessens the "utter courtesy" of the service performed for the knight by making menial service the patrician maiden's "wont;" whereas the lines added in the '59 edition describing the unwillingness of the Prince to allow so sweet a high-born maid to perform so menial a task and his refraining from himself performing this task, from "utter courtesy," "reverencing the custom of the house," forbearing to wound the pride of the fallen Earl,— these add greatly to the beauty of the scene, as does also the omission of the line in the '57 copy amplifying the details in regard to the care of the knight's horse, the stable service of feeding and of littering him, though, indeed, some previous experience of this sort might not come amiss in enabling Enid to "drive on before her" the *twelve* horses, which, according to the "Mabinogion," Geraint won that day. Even thus her success was but moderate. "And it grieved him as much as his wrath would permit, to see a maiden so illustrious as she having so much trouble with the care of the horses."

'57. A youth, that following *in* a costrel bore
'59. A youth, that following *with* a costrel bore (100, 10.)

K.   I am Geraint
  Of Droon—for this morning when the Queen
'57.   I am Geraint
  Of Devon—for this morning when the Queen
             (101, 7.)

'57. *For but to hear of these is grateful to us*
  Who see but acts of *violence;* such a pair
  Of suitors *had* this maiden;
MS. *So grateful is the noise of noble deeds*
  To those who suffer wrong, & such a pair
  Of suitors *had* this maiden;
'59. *So grateful is the noise of noble deeds*
  To noble hearts who see but acts of *wrong:*
  O never yet had woman such a pair
  Of suitors *as* this maiden; (102, 9.)

In '59 the "pair of suitors" are introduced more skilfully. In reading the '57 copy the mind halts at the line, "such a pair of suitors had this maiden," in the effort to recollect where this pair of suitors was described, but in the '59 form of statement the mind runs on to the description following without effort.

K. And *placed* me in this ruinous castle here,
'57. And *keeps* me in this ruinous castle here, (103, 7.)

'57. That if, *as I suppose, your* nephew fights
'69. That if *the sparrow-hawk, this* nephew, fight (103, 20.)

'57. Two forks are fixt into the meadow ground,
And over these is *laid* a silver wand,
And over that *is placed the* sparrow-hawk,
'73. Two forks are fixt into the meadow ground,
And over these is *placed* a silver wand,
And over that *a golden* sparrow-hawk, (104, 2.)

'57. (Who hearing her own name had *slipt* away)
'84. (Who hearing her own name had *stol'n* away) (105, 2.)

'57. Beheld her *there before him in the field*
'59. Beheld her *first in field, awaiting him*, (106, 9.)

In the '57 version "there before him" is, perhaps, intended as an adverbial element of place,

and when Geraint
Beheld her there before him in the field
He felt, were she the prize of bodily force,
Himself beyond the rest pushing could move
The chair of Idris.

THE BEGINNINGS OF THE IDYLLS. 71

though the expression may be taken as an adverbial element of time. There is no obscurity in the '59 line.

'57. And over these they placed *a* silver wand,
And over that *a* golden sparrow-hawk.
'73. And over these they placed *the* silver wand,
And over that *the* golden sparrow-hawk. (106, 18.)

In the '57 copy the two accounts of fixing the forks into the ground and placing in position the silver wand and the sparrow-hawk (104, 2, and 106, 18) seem to be independent. The second account describes the placing of *a* silver wand and of *a* golden sparrow-hawk. (The first account does not make the sparrow-hawk "golden.") But in '73 the sparrow-hawk is called "golden" in the first description, and in the second description we have no longer *a* silver wand and *a* golden sparrow-hawk, but *the* silver wand and *the* golden sparrow-hawk. That is, the two accounts are now associated in the poet's mind.

'57. *For* I these two years past have won *it* for thee,
'86. *What* I these two years past have won for thee,
(106, 23.)
'57. And crack*t* the *skull-cap* thro', and bit the bone,
'59. And crack'*d* the *helmet* thro,' and bit the bone,
(107, 16.)
'57. First, thou thyself, *thy lady, and thy* dwarf,
Shalt ride to Arthur's court, and *being* there,
'73. First, thou thyself, *with damsel and with* dwarf,
Shalt ride to Arthur's court, and *coming* there,
(107, 24.)

The companion of the sparrow-hawk, here called
lady in '57 and *damsel* in '73, is in '93 still designated
as a *lady* on p. 92, 1. 11, p. 104, 1. 7, and p. 106, 1. 21.

'57. And being young, he changed *himself, and grew
To hate the sin that seem'd so like his own
Of Modred, Arthur's nephew*, and fell at last
In the great battle fighting for the king.
'69. And being young, he changed *and came to loathe
His crime of traitor, slowly drew himself
Bright from his old dark life*, and fell at last
In the great battle fighting for the king. (108, 11.)

'57. Sweet heavens, how much I shall discredit him!
Would he *but* tarry with us *a day or two;*
'59. Sweet heaven, how much I shall discredit him!
Would he *could* tarry with us *here awhile!* (109, 13.)

'57. Yet if he *would* but *rest* a day or two,
Myself would work *my fingers to the bone*,
Far *rather* than so much discredit him.'
'59. Yet if he *could* but *tarry* a day or two,
Myself would work *eye dim, and finger lame*,
Far *liefer* than so much discredit him.' (109, 19.)

'57. And answer'd, ' *Yea*, I know it; your good gift,
MS. And answer'd, ' *Oh*, I know it; your good gift,
'59. And answer'd, ' *Yea*, I know it; your good gift,
(112, 4.)

'57. But since our fortune *slipt* from sun to shade,
'84. But since our fortune *swerved* from sun to shade,
(113, 3.)

K. And should some great court-lady say, the Prince
Hath pick*t* a *pretty beggar* from the hedge,
And like a madman brought her to the court,

'59. And should some great court-lady say, the Prince
Hath pick'd a *ragged-robin* from the hedge,
And like a madman brought her to the court,
(113, 12.)

"In an early 'Calendar of English Flowers' we are told that 'Poor Ragged Robin blossoms in the haie' (hedge). It is a red wildflower, also called Cuckoo-flower, and is common in English hedgerows; but when Enid's mother speaks of a Ragged Robin from the hedge, she is thinking less of the literal wildflower than of a ragged beggar-girl from the roadside."—Littledale, " Essays on Lord Tennyson's Idylls of the King," p. 132. Macmillan & Co., London, 1893.

In determining whether or no the change is for us an improvement, we should, perhaps, recall the words with which Guinevere sent Geraint forth on his adventure,

'Farewell, fair Prince,' answer'd the stately Queen.
'Be prosperous in this journey, as in all;
And may you light on all things that you love,
And live to wed with her whom first you love:
But ere you wed with any, bring your bride,
And I, were she the daughter of a king,
Yea, *tho' she were a beggar from the hedge,*
Will clothe her for her bridals like the sun.'

In the following there are three *buts* in close proximity in the South Kensington copy (the second of these is changed to *and* in '57), and there is uncertainty as to punctuation in all the early copies. In

the South Kensington "Enid" there is a quotation
mark before *Whom* in the second line, in '57 it is
placed before *Flur*, in '59 it is omitted altogether and
a comma is placed after *we* in the line before the last.
In '73 the lines are as in '92.

    K. And call'd her like that maiden in the tale,
       'Whom Gwydion made by glamour out of flowers,
       And sweeter than the bride of Cassivelaun,
       Flur, for whose love the Roman Cæsar first
       Invaded Britain, but we beat him back,
       As this great prince invaded us, *but* we
       Not beat him back, but welcomed him with joy.
                                 (114, 6.)

 '57. Laid from her limbs the costly-*braided* gift,
 '59. Laid from her limbs the costly-*broider'd* gift,
                                    (115, 7.)

 '57. Thereafter, when I reach'd this ruin'd *hold*,
       Beholding one so bright in dark estate,
       I vow'd that could I gain her, our *kind* Queen,
 '73. Thereafter, when I reach'd this ruin'd *hall*,
       Beholding one so bright in dark estate,
       I vow'd that could I gain her, our *fair* Queen,
                                    (115, 23.)

K.   for I wish the two
       To love each other. Enid cannot find
       A nobler friend: *another* thought I had,
 '57.   for I wish the two
       To love each other; Enid *cannot* find
       A nobler friend. *Another* thought I had;
 '59.   *for I wish* the two
       To love each other: *how should* Enid find
       A nobler friend? Another thought *I had*;

'73.   *fain I would* the two
   Should love each other: *how can* Enid find
   A nobler friend? Another thought *was mine;*
                                                    (116, 3.)

K. I came among you here so suddenly,
   I told my love for her so suddenly,
   That tho' her gentle presence at the lists
   Might well have served for proof that I was loved,
   I doubted whether *filial softness in her,*
   Or *waxen* nature *had* not let itself
   Be moulded by your wishes for her weal— (116, 6.)

In '57 the second line, "I told my love for her so suddenly," is omitted and Enid's "waxen" nature becomes her "easy" nature. In '59 for the "filial softness in her" of '57 we have "filial tenderness," which in '73 becomes "daughter's tenderness." In '57 we have "had," in '59 "did," and in '73 "might" not let itself be moulded by your wishes for her weal.

K. And *that same* sense might make her long for court
'57. And *such a* sense might make her long for court

K. And all its *dangerous* glories; and I thought,
'73. And all its *perilous* glories: and I thought,

'57. That could I someway prove *that* force in her
'59. That could I someway prove *such* force in her

K. Of intermitted *custom,* then I felt
'73. Of intermitted *usage;* then I felt
MS.   then I *knew*
   That I could rest a rock in ebbs and flows,
   Fixt on her faith: (116, 23.)

There are nine pages in Tennyson concerning the wearing of the faded silk to court, seven lines in the "Mabinogion." "Where is the Earl Ynywl," said Geraint, "and his wife, and his daughter?" "They are in the chamber yonder," said the Earl's chamberlain, "arraying themselves in garments which the Earl has caused to be brought for them." "Let the damsel not array herself," said he, "except in her vest and her veil, until she come to the Court of Arthur, to be clad by Gwenhwyvar, in such garments as she may choose." So the maiden did not array herself. p. 152.

'57.   Grant me pardon for my thoughts,
*I have not kept them long. I promise you
That when we come once more, as come we shall,
To see you, she* shall wear your *noble* gift,
Here at your own warm hearth, with, on her knee,
Who knows? another gift of the high God,
Which maybe shall have learn'd to lisp you thanks.'
Then smiled the mother, pleased, and half in tears
*To hear him talk so solemnly and well:
And* brought a mantle down and wrapt her in it,
And claspt and kiss'd her, and they rode away.

MS.   Grant me pardon for my thoughts,
I have not kept them long. *I pledge my faith
That Enid, when we come, some golden day,
As come we will,* shall wear your noble gift,
Here at your own warm hearth, with, on her knee,
Who knows? another gift of the high God,

.   .   .   .

And claspt and kiss'd her, and they rode away.

'59.   Grant me pardon for my thoughts:
And for my strange petition I will make

Amends hereafter by some gaudy-day,
When your fair child shall wear your *costly* gift
Beside your own warm hearth, with, on her knees,
Who knows? another gift of the high God,
Which, maybe, shall have learn'd to lisp you thanks.'
He spoke: the mother smiled, but half in tears,
Then brought a mantle down and wrapt her in it,
And claspt and kiss'd her, and they rode away.
(117, 1.)

K.   Now *on* that morning Guinevere had climb'd
The *summit of that* tower from *which* they say
Men saw the goodly hills of Somerset,
'57.   Now *on* that morning Guinevere had climb'd
The *giant* tower from *whose high crest* they say
Men saw the goodly hills of Somerset, (117, 11.)

In '59 " Now *on* that morning" becomes " Now *thrice* that morning."

K.   O purblind race of miserable men,
How many among us at this very hour
Do forge a life-long trouble for *th*emselves,
By taking *false* for *true,* or *true* for *false;*
'57.   O purblind race of miserable men,
How many among us at this very hour
Do forge a life-long trouble for *our*selves,
By taking *true* for *false,* or *false* for *true;*   (119, 1.)

'59. *Round was their pace at first, but slacken'd soon:*
'57. (Not in '57).   (120, 21.)

'57. In shadow, waiting for them, *varlets* all;
'59. In shadow, waiting for them, *caitiffs* all;   (121, 20.)

'57.   ' Did I wish
Your *silence* or your *warning?*

'69.   ' Did I wish
      Your *warning* or your *silence?* (122, 13.)

Doubtless it was the influence of his source which led the poet into this error. In the "Mabinogion," p. 164, Geraint says, "I wish but for silence, and not for warning." And this is the correct order for a declarative sentence. But when the sentence was put into the interrogative form, it was necessary to change the order of *silence* and *warning*, if it was desired to imply the answer by the form of the question. And yet not until '69 do we have

              Did I wish
      Your warning or your silence?

K. Swung from his brand a windy buffet out
   Once *more* to right, to left, and *stunn'd* the twain
   Or slew them,
'57. Swung from his brand a windy buffet out
   Once, *twice*, to right, to left, and *stun'd* the twain
   Or slew them,   (123, 3.)

'57. And all in charge of *a mere* girl : set on.'
'59. And all in charge of *whom?* a girl : set on.' (124, 13.)

'57. That had a sapling growing on it, *slip*
'73. That had a sapling growing on it, *slide* (126, 1.)

K. And I *am also* his; and I will tell him
'57. And I *myself am* his; and I will tell him (128, 16.)

'57. And *stabling* for the horses, and return
'59. And *stalling* for the horses, and return (129, 2.)

K. Then *mark'd* the mowers labouring dinnerless,
'57. Then *with another humourous ruth remark'd*
  The *lusty* mowers labouring dinnerless, (129, 13.)
K. She answer'd, 'Thanks, my lord:' *they rested mute,*
  Like creatures voiceless *from* the fault of birth,
  Or two wild men supporters of a shield
  Painted, who stare at open space, nor glance
  The one at other, parted by the shield,
  And sunder'd by the whole breadth of the room.
'57. She answer'd, 'Thanks, my lord:' *they two remain'd,*
  Divided by the chamber's width and mute
  As creatures voiceless *by* the fault of birth,
  Or two wild men supporters of a shield,
  Painted, who stare at open space, nor glance
  The one at other, parted by the shield.
'59. She answer'd, 'Thanks, my lord;' *the two remain'd*
  Apart by all the chamber's width, and mute
  As creatures voiceless *thro'* the fault of birth,
  Or two wild men supporters of a shield,
  Painted, who stare at open space, nor glance
  The one at other, parted by the shield. (130, 2.)

K. Then *call'd* Geraint for wine and goodly cheer
  To feed the sudden guest, and Earl Limours
  Drank till he jested with all ease,
'57. Then *call'd* Geraint for wine and goodly cheer
  To feed the sudden guest, *and bad the host*
  Call in what men soever were his friends,
  And feast with these in honour of their earl;
  '*And care not for the cost; the cost is mine.*'
  And wine and food were brought, and Earl Limours
  Drank till he jested with all ease,
'59. Then *cried* Geraint for wine and goodly cheer
  To feed the sudden guest, and *sumptuously*
  According to his fashion. bad the host

>   Call in what men soever were his friends,
>   And feast with these in honour of their earl;
>   'And care not for the cost; the cost is mine.'
>   And wine and food were brought, and Earl Limours
>   Drank till he jested with all ease, (130, 21.)

K.   thus he moved the Prince
>   To laughter and his *menay* to applause.
'57.   thus he moved the Prince
>   To laughter and his *comrades* to applause. (131. 7.)

K. And when the Prince was merry, ask'd Limours
>   '*Have I* your leave, my lord, to cross, and speak
>   To your good damsel there who sits apart
'57. Then, when the Prince was merry, ask'd Limours,
>   'Your leave, my lord, to cross *the room*, and speak
>   To your good damsel there who sits apart, (131, 9.)

K. Like *one that* tries *new* ice if it will bear,
'57. Like *one* that tries *old* ice if it will bear,
'59. Like *him who* tries *the bridge he fears may fail,*
>   (131, 15.)

K. I thought, but that your father came between,
>   In former days you saw me favourably:
>   And if it were so do not keep it back.
>   Owe you me nothing for a life half-lost?
>   Yea, yea, the whole dear debt of all you are.
'57. I thought, but that your father came between,
>   In former days you saw me favourably.
>   And if it were so do not keep it back:
>   *Make me a little happier: let me know it:*
>   Owe you me nothing for a life half-lost?
>   Yea, yea, the whole dear debt of all you are.
>   (131, 26.)

THE BEGINNINGS OF THE IDYLLS. 81

'57. And, Enid, you and he, I see *it* with joy—
'73. And, Enid, you and he, I see with joy, (132, 6.)

K.   and your wretched dress,
    A wretched insult on you, dumbly *shrieks*
    Your story, that this man loves you no more.
    Your beauty is *to him beauty no more.*
'57.   and your wretched dress,
    A wretched insult on you, dumbly *speaks*
    Your story, that this man loves you no more.
    Your beauty is *no beauty to him now:* (132, 13.)

K. *You* need *not* look so scared at what I say :
'57. *Nor* need *you* look so scared at what I say : (132, 25.)

'57. The one true lover *which* you ever *had,*
'73. The one true lover *whom* you ever *own'd,* (133, 4.)

'57. *To-night I am quite weary and worn out.'*
'59. *Leave me to-night: I am weary to the death.'* (133, 18.)

K. Anon she rose and stepping lightly heap'd
    The pieces of his armour in one place
    To be at hand against a sudden need,
'57. Anon she rose and stepping lightly heap'd
    The pieces of his armour in one place,
    All to be there against a sudden need; (134, 9.)

K. That tho' he thought 'was it for him she wept
    In Devon?' he but gave *an angry* groan,
    Saying 'your sweet faces make good fellows fools
    And traitors; call the host and bid him bring
    My charger and *your* palfrey.' *Enid went:*
    He arm'd, and issuing found the host and cried,

'Your reckoning, friend?' and ere he learnt it, 'Take
Five horses and their armours,' *then* the host
Amazed, 'I have not spent the worth of one.'
'You will be all the wealthier' *cried* the Prince.
'57. That tho' he thought, 'was it for him she wept
In Devon?' he but gave *a wrathful* groan,
Saying 'your sweet faces make good fellows fools
And traitors. Call the host and bid him bring
Charger and palfrey.' *So she glided out
Among the heavy breathings of the house,
And like a household spirit at the walls
Beat, till she woke the sleepers, and return'd:
Then tho' he had not ask'd her, tending him
In silence, did him service as a squire;
Till issuing arm'd he* found the host and cried,
'Your reckoning, friend,' and ere he learnt it, 'Take
Five horses and their armours;' *and* the host,
Suddenly honest, answer'd in amaze,
'*My lord*, I have not spent the worth of one!'
'You will be all the wealthier' *said* the Prince,'
(135, 6.)

'57. Then *tho' he had not ask'd her,* tending *him*
'59. Then tending *her rough lord, tho' all unask'd,* (135, 14.)

'57. 'My lord, I *have not* spent the worth of one!'
'59. 'My lord, I *scarce have* spent the worth of one!'
(135, 20.)

'57. That whatsoever thing you see or hear
'59. What thing soever you may hear, or see, (135, 24.)

'57. Not *quite* mismated with a yawning clown,
'73. Not *all* mismated with a yawning clown, (136, 9.)

K. And that within her which *an easy* fool
    Or hasty judger would have called her guilt,

'57. And that within her which *a wanton fool*
   Or hasty judger would have call'd her guilt, (136, 15.)

K. Dash'd on Geraint, who *hurtled* with him and bore
'57. Dash'd on Geraint, who *closed* with him, and bore
                                                    (137, 21.)
'57. But if a man who stands upon the *bank*
'59. But if a man who stand upon the *brink* (138, 5.)

K.   Then like a stormy sunlight smiled Geraint,
   Who saw the chargers of the two that fell
   Start *masterless* from their *mute* lords and fly,
   Mixt with the flyers. '*Honest friends!*' he said,
   '*Almost* as honest as a weeping wife.
   Not a hoof left!
'57.   Then like a stormy sunlight smiled Geraint,
   Who saw the chargers of the two that fell
   Start from their *fallen* lords, and *wildly* fly,
   Mixt with the flyers. '*Horse and man*,' he said,
   '*All of one mind and all right-honest friends!*
   Wellnigh as honest as a weeping wife;
   Not a hoof left: (138, 13.)

Omitted in '59.
   '*Wellnigh as honest as a weeping wife;*

K. What say you *therefore?* shall we strip him there
'57. *And so* what say you? shall we strip him there
                                                    (138, 21.)
K. Nor let her true hand falter *or her* eye
   Moisten, till she had lighted on his wound,
'57. Nor let her true hand falter, *nor blue* eye
   Moisten, till she had lighted on his wound, (139, 19.)

K. Another past, a *whistling* man-at-arms
   Bound on a mission to the bandit earl,
   And drove the dust against her veilless eyes;

'57. Another *hurried* past, a man-at-arms
  Bound on a mission to the bandit earl,
  Half whistling and half singing a coarse song,
  And drove the dust against her veilless eyes :
MS. Another *pass'd*, a man-at-arms, *who rode*
  Bound on a mission to the bandit earl,
  Half whistling and half singing a coarse song,
'59. Another *hurrying* past, a man-at-arms,
  Rode on a mission to the bandit Earl ;
  Half whistling and half singing a coarse song,
  He drove the dust against her veilless eyes: (140, 9.)

K.   Then said Earl Doorm, 'Well, if he be not dead,
  Why wail you for him thus? you seem a child;
  And *if he be* dead, I count you for a fool,
  Your wailing will not *help* him : *either way*
  You *spoil* a comely face with *crying for him.*
'57.   Then said Earl Doorm ; 'Well, if he be not dead,
  Why wail you for him thus? you seem a child.
  And *be he* dead, I count you for a fool ;
  Your wailing will not *quicken* him : *dead or not,*
  You *mar* a comely face with *idiot tears.* (141, 4.)

'57. (His gentle charger following *all* unled)
  And laid him on a settle in the hall,
'59. (His gentle charger following *him* unled)
  *And cast him and the bier in which he lay
  Down on an oaken* settle in the hall, (142, 4.)

"The Earl caused the knight that was dead to be buried, but he thought that there still remained some life in Geraint ; and to see if he would live, he had him carried with him in the hollow of his shield, and *upon a bier.*"—The "Mabinogion," p. 179.

K. And out of her there *flow'd* a power upon him,
'57. And out of her there *came* a power upon him; (143, 21.)

K. *For*, I myself, when flush'd with fight, or hot,
'57. *Lo!* I, myself, when flush'd with fight, or hot, (145, 16.)

K.   He spoke, and one among his gentlewomen
Display'd a splendid silk of *costliest* loom,
'57.   He spoke, and one among his gentlewomen
Display'd a splendid silk of *foreign* loom, (146, 19.)

The word *foreign* is used in the same sense in the "Mabinogion," p. 163. "Then went Geraint to the place where his horse was, and it was equipped with *foreign* armour, heavy and shining."

'57. She only prayed him, ' Fly *my lord at once
Before these thieves return and murder you.*
Your charger is without, my palfrey lost
For ever.' 'Then,' *he answered*, 'shall you ride
Behind me.'
'59. She only prayed him, ' Fly, *they will return
And slay you; fly*, your charger is without,
My palfrey lost.' 'Then, *Enid*, shall you ride
Behind me.' (149, 5.)

K. With a low *whining* towards the pair:
'57. With a low *whinny* towards the pair:
'59. With a low whinny toward the pair: (149, 13.)

'57.   then Geraint upon the horse
Mounted, and *lent an arm*, and on his foot
She set her own and climb'd;
'59.   then Geraint upon the horse
Mounted, and *reach'd a hand*, and on his foot
She set her own and climb'd; (149, 15.)

In the '57 copy *an arm* is crossed out and *a hand* is written above; then the whole is crossed out and *reach'd a hand* written instead, which we find in '59.

    K. Than Enid *felt*, who in that perilous hour
  '57. Than Enid *proved*,
  MS. Than *lived thro' her*,
  '59. Than lived thro' her,

  MS.   And never yet, since high in Paradise
        O'er the four rivers the first roses blew,
        Came purer pleasure unto mortal kind
        Than *lived thro' her*, who in that perilous hour
        Put hand to hand beneath her husband's heart,
        And felt him hers again : ∧ she did not weep,
                        she could not speak, [Written on
        Not even to her own self in silent words,   margin
        And shadows of a sound :   below]
        But o'er her meek eyes came a happy mist
        Like that which kept the heart of Eden green
        Before the useful trouble of the rain : (149, 23.)

Stopford A. Brooke speaks of these as " some of the loveliest lines he ever wrote of womanhood." Each reader will doubtless prefer to judge for himself whether or no these " loveliest lines" would have been bettered by the adoption of the proposed addition.

  '57. Was half a bandit in my lawless *days*,
  '59. Was half a bandit in my lawless *hour*, (150, 27.)

    K. I come the mouthpiece of our king to Doorm
       (The king is close behind me), bidding him
       Disband himself, and scatter all his powers,
       Submitting to the judgment of the king.'
       Doorm is disbanded by the King of Fears,

THE BEGINNINGS OF THE IDYLLS. 87

And suffers judgment from the King of Kings,'
Cried the wan Prince;
'57. I come the mouthpiece of our king to Doorm
(The king is close behind me), bidding him
Disband himself, and scatter all his powers
Submitting to the judgment of the king.'
' *He hath submitted to* the King of Kings,'
Cried the wan Prince;
'59. I come the mouthpiece of our King to Doorm
(The King is close behind me) bidding him
Disband himself, and scatter all his powers,
Submit, and hear the judgment of the King.'
' *He hears the judgment of* the King of Kings,'
Cried the wan Prince; (151, 1.)

K. ' Fair and dear cousin, fear *not*, I am changed.
'57. ' Fair and dear cousin, *you that most had cause
To fear me*, fear *no longer*, I am changed. (152, 4.)

K.   being repulsed
By Yniol and yourself, I *plotted*, wrought
Until I overturn'd him;
'57.   being repulsed
By Yniol and yourself, I *schemed and* wrought
Until I overturn'd him; (152, 8.)

K. *I think* I should have killed him. And you came,—
'57. *I think* I should *not less* have kill'd him. And you came,—
'59. I should not less have kill'd him. And you came,—
            (152, 25.)

Evidently *not less* was written on some proof-sheet and the *I think* not crossed out. The '57 line, therefore, contains twelve syllables. In the passage following there is an error in the tense of a verb in the '57 copy, *know* in the fifth line.

K. And all the penance the Queen laid upon me
   Was but to rest awhile within her court.
   First was I sullen, like a beast new caged,
   And waiting to be treated like a wolf,
   Because *they knew my doings; but* I found,
   Instead of scornful pity or pure scorn,
'57. And all the penance the Queen laid upon me
   Was but to rest awhile within her court.
   Where first all-sullen, like a beast new-caged,
   And waiting to be treated like a wolf,
   Because *I know they knew my deeds,* I found,
   Instead of scornful pity or pure scorn,
'59. And all the penance the Queen laid upon me
   Was but to rest awhile within her court;
   Where first *as sullen as* a beast new-caged,
   And waiting to be treated like a wolf,
   Because *I knew my deeds were known,* I found,
   Instead of scornful pity or pure scorn, (153, 8.)

K. *But* fear not, cousin; I am changed indeed.'
'57. But *kept myself aloof till I was changed;*
   And fear not, cousin; I am changed indeed.' (153, 27.)

'57.   but now behold me come
   To cleanse this common *shore* of all my realm,
'59.   but now behold me come
   To cleanse this common *sewer* of all my realm, (154, 21.)

K. The king's own *leach* to look into his hurt,
'57. The king's own *leech* to look into his hurt; (155, 24.)

'57. On *whom his father* Uther left in charge
'69. On *each of all whom* Uther left in charge (156, 9.)

K. He look'd and found them wanting, and as men
   Weed the white horse *upon* the Berkshire hills

'57. He look'd and found them wanting; and as *now*
    Men weed the white horse on the Berkshire hills
                                                (156, 11.)
'57. And fifty knights rode with them to the *ford*
    Of Severn, and they past to their own land.
'59. And fifty knights rode with them to the *shores*
    Of Severn, and they past to their own land.
                                                (157, 6.)
'57. A happy life with a fair death, and fell
    At Longport, fighting for the blameless king.
'59. A happy life with a fair death, and fell
    Against the heathen of the Northern Sea
    In battle, fighting for the blameless King. (157, 20.)

The earlier copy, which says of Geraint that he "fell at Longport," is closer to the original. In the notes to the "Mabinogion" we have quoted from "the beautiful Elegy composed on him by his fellow-warrior, the venerable bard Llywarch Hên,"

   At *Llongborth* was Geraint slain,
   A valiant warrior from the woodlands of Devon,
   Slaughtering his foes as he fell.

* NIMUË.

'57. A storm was coming, but the winds were still,
    And in the wild woods of Broceliande,

---

* Where we have *Vivien* in '59 we have uniformly *Nimuë* in '57.

The MS. corrections given under *Nimuë* are found in the South Kensington copy, not in the British Museum copy.

Before an oak so hollow huge and old
It look'd a tower of *ruin'd* masonwork,
At Merlin's feet the *wileful Nimuë* lay.
   The *wileful Nimuë* stole from Arthur's court:
She hated all the knights *because she deem'd*
They wink'd and jested when her name was named.
For once when Arthur, walking all alone
* *And troubled in his heart* about the Queen,
Had met her, *she had spoken to the King*
With reverent eyes, mock-loyal shaken voice,
And fluttered adoration, and at last
Had hinted at the some who prized him more
Than who should prize him most: at which the King
Had gazed upon her blankly and gone by;

'59. A storm was coming, but the winds were still,
And in the wild woods of Broceliande,
Before an oak, so hollow huge and old
It look'd a tower of *ruin'd* masonwork,
At Merlin's feet the *wily Vivien* lay.
   The *wily Vivien* stole from Arthur's court:
She hated all the knights, *and heard in thought*
Their lavish comment when her name was named.
For once, when Arthur walking all alone,
Vext at a rumour rife about the Queen,
Had met her, *Vivien, being greeted fair,*
Would fain have wrought upon his cloudy mood
With reverent eyes mock-loyal, shaken voice,
And flutter'd adoration, and at last
With dark sweet hints of some who prized him more
Than who should prize him most; at which the King
Had gazed upon her blankly and gone by:

---

* See the discussion in regard to the omission of this line.

THE BEGINNINGS OF THE IDYLLS. 91

'74. A storm was coming, but the winds were still,
And in the wild woods of Broceliande,
Before an oak, so hollow, huge and old
It look'd a tower of *ruin'd* masonwork,
At Merlin's feet the wily Vivien lay.
 Whence came she? One that bare in bitter grudge
The scorn of Arthur and his Table, Mark
The Cornish King, had heard a wandering voice,
A minstrel of Caerleon by strong storm
Blown into shelter at Tintagil, etc.
 (six pages here closing with the line)
The wily Vivien stole from Arthur's court.
 She hated all the knights, and heard in thought
Their lavish comment when her name was named.
For once, when Arthur walking all alone,
Vext at a rumour *issued from herself*
Of some corruption crept among his knights,
 (then as in '59) (182, 3.)

In '86 *ruin'd* masonwork becomes *ivied* masonwork, and the *scorn* of Mark becomes the *slights* of Mark.

The visit of a harper to the court of Mark (described in the six pages added to "Vivien" in '74) may have been suggested by Malory (Book X., chapter xxvii.). Mark had received some letters brought by a "damosell." "Damosell," said king Marke, "will yee ride and beare letters from mee unto king Arthur?" "Sir," said shee, "I will bee at your commandement for to ride when yee will." Sir Tristram and Mark's wife, La beale Isoud, gave the "damosell" directions to come to them before starting for Arthur's court, "that wee may see the privity of your letters." Marke's suspicions were, perhaps, aroused, for on the morrow he said to the "damosell," "I am not advised at this time to send my letters." He, however, "prively" sent letters to queene Guenever, sir Launcelot, and king Arthur; "and the beginning of the kings letter spake wondrous short unto King Arthur." The letters to queene Guenever and sir Launcelot made them also "wroth out of measure." But sir Dinadan comforted sir Launcelot with this "counsaile": "I will make a lay for him, and when it is made, I shall make an harper to sing it before him." "And so by the will of sir Launcelot and of king Arthur, the harpers went straight unto Wales and Cornewaile, to sing the lay that sir Dinadan made by king Marke, *which was the worst lay that ever harper sung with harpe or with any other instrument.*" (Malory is "vague and uncommunicative on the subject of the so-called lay. We know, however, from the story current in Wales and Ireland that the burden of it was nothing more or less than this: King Mark has horse's ears."—Professor Rhys, "Studies in the Arthurian Legend," p. 358.)

One may premise that after the singing of this "lay," Marke, in Malory as in Tennyson, was

> half in heart to hurl his cup
> Straight at the speaker,

for Malory says, "But for to say that king Marke was wondrous wroth, hee was." "'I charge that thou hie thee fast out of my sight' said he to the harper."

'57. She play'd about with slight and sprightly talk;
And yielding to his kindlier moods, the Seer
'59. She play'd about with slight and sprightly talk,
*And vivid smiles, and faintly-venom'd points
Of slander, glancing here and grazing there;*
And yielding to his kindlier moods, the Seer (189, 10.)

'57. Tolerant of what he half disdain'd, and she
Began to break her sports with graver fits,
'59. Tolerant of what he half disdain'd, and she,
Perceiving that she was but half disdain'd,
Began to break her sports with graver fits, (189, 17.)

'57. Fixt in her will, and so the seasons went.
Then fell *upon him* a great melancholy,
And leaving Arthur's court he gained the beach;
'73. Fixt in her will, and so the seasons went.
Then fell *on Merlin* a great melancholy;
*He walk'd with dreams and darkness, and he found
A doom that ever poised itself to fall,
An ever-moaning battle in the mist,
World-war of dying flesh against the life,
Death in all life and lying in all love,
The meanest having power upon the highest,
And the high purpose broken by the worm.*
So leaving Arthur's court he gain'd the beach;
(189, 27.)

'57. *I look'd, and when I* saw you following still,
'59. *And when I look'd, and* saw you following still, (194, 6.)

'57. That I should prove it on you unawares,
To make you lose your use and name and fame,

That makes me *too indignant.* Then our bond
Had best be loosed for ever:
'59. That I should prove it on your unawares,
To make you lose your use and name and fame,
That makes me *most indignant;* then our bond
Had best be loosed for ever:
'73. That I should prove it on you unawares,
That makes me *passing wrathful;* then our bond
Had best be loosed for ever: (195, 21.)

K. And then was painting on it fancied arms,
An Eagle, noir in azure, volant, armed
Gules; and a scroll beneath 'I follow fame.'
MS. And then was painting on it fancied arms,
A golden Eaglet on an azure field,
Volant in bend; the scroll 'I follow fame.'
'59. And then was painting on it fancied arms,
Azure, an Eagle rising or, the Sun
In dexter chief; the scroll "I follow fame." (201, 5.)

'57. Because I *wish'd to give* them greater *minds:*
'73. Because I *fain had given* them greater *wits:* (201, 25.)

K. *Right well know I* that Fame is half-disfame,
MS. *Who knew right well* that Fame is half-disfame, (202, 8.)

Then the whole line as amended was crossed out
and afterward marked *stet.*

'57.   a single misty star,
That [*Which* '59] is the second in a line of stars
That seem a sword beneath a belt of three,

K. (*As sons of kings loving* in pupillage
Have turn'd to tyrants when they *came* to power)
MS. (*As royal children, sweet* in pupillage,
May turn to tyrants when they *come* to power) (202, 21.)

THE BEGINNINGS OF THE IDYLLS. 95

The lines were then crossed out and later marked *stet* and given in '59 as in '57.

'57. And being found take heed of *Nimuë then.*
'59. And being found take heed of *Vivien.* (203, 6.)

'57. Without the *whole* heart back may merit well
'59. Without the *full* heart back may merit well
(203, 11.)

'57. You cage a *pretty* captive here and there,
'59. You cage a *buxom* captive here and there, (203, 19.)

'57. The feet *unsolder'd* from their ancle-bones
'59. The feet *unmortised* from their an*k*le-bones (204, 4.)

'57. The king impaled him for his piracy;
Then made her Queen: but those isle-nurtur'd eyes
Made such unwilling tho' successful war
On all the youth, they sicken'd; (204, 21.)

In the South Kensington Museum "Nimuë" the first *made* is crossed out and *crown'd* written instead, but in '59 the first made is retained and the second made changed to *waged*.

'57. And beasts themselves *did homage;* camels knelt
Unbidden, and the *beasts* of mountain *bulk*
That carry kings in castles, bow'd black knees
Of homage,
'59. And beasts themselves *would worship;* camels knelt
Unbidden, and the *brutes* of mountain *back*
That carry kings in castles, bow'd black knees
Of homage, (205, 1.)

'57.   she had her pleasure in it.
      And lived there neither dame nor damsel then
'59.   she had her pleasure in it,
      And made her good man jealous with good cause.
      And lived there neither dame nor damsel then
                                          (206, 4.)

'57. Well those were *ancient* days: but did they find
      A wizard? Tell me, was he like to thee?
      '*No.*' *And she* made her lithe arm round his neck
'59. Well, those were *not our* days: but did they find
      A wizard? Tell me, was he like to thee?
      She ceased, and made her lithe arm round his neck
                                        (206, 12.)

'57. *Who thinks* her new lord *is* the first of men.
      He answer'd laughing, 'Nay, not like to me.
'59. *On* her new lord, *her own,* the first of men.
      He answer'd laughing, 'Nay, not like to me.
                                      (206, 17.)

'57. '*The filthy swine! what do they* say of me?
'59. '*What dare the full-fed liars* say of me? (209, 16.)

'57. Not one of *them* should touch me: *filthy* swine!'
'59. Not one of *all the drove* should touch me: swine!'
                                      (209, 23.)

'57. Some cause had kept him *separate* from his wife.
'59. Some cause had kept him *sunder'd* from his wife:
                                    (210, 14.)

'57. And Merlin answer'd, 'Overquick are you
      To catch a *filthy* plume fall'n from the wing (211, 1.)

In the South Kensington "Nimuë', there is a MS. correction of *filthy* to *loathsome*. Then *loathsome* is changed to *lothly*, and in '73 to *loathly*.

THE BEGINNINGS OF THE IDYLLS. 97

'57. And wearied out *crept* to the couch and slept
'59. And wearied out *made for* the couch and slept,
(211, 11.)
'57.   that commerce with the Queen,
I ask you, is it *patent to* the child,
'59.   that commerce with the Queen,
I ask you, is it *clamour'd by* the child, (212, 20.)

'57. Sir Lancelot went ambassador, at first,
To fetch her, and she took him for the king;
So fixt her fancy on him; let *him* be.
'73. Sir Lancelot went ambassador, at first,
To fetch her, and she *watch'd him from her walls.*
A rumour runs, she took him for the King,
So fixt her fancy on him: let *them* be (212, 24.)

'57. '*Him?* is he man at all, who knows and winks?
'73. '*Man!* is he man at all, who knows and winks?
(213, 7.)
'57. *I think* she cloaks the *wounds of loss* with lies;
I do believe she tempted them and fail'd,
She is so bitter:
'73. She cloaks the *scar of some repulse* with lies;
I *well* believe she tempted them and fail'd,
Being so bitter: (214, 19.)

'57. Then her false voice made way broken with sobs.
'*Cruel, the love that I have wasted on you!*
O cruel, there was nothing wild or strange,
Or seeming shameful, for what shame in *trust,*
So love be true, and not as yours is—nothing
Poor *Nimuë* had not done to *pleasure him*
Who call'd her what he call'd her—all her crime,
The master-wish to prove him wholly hers.'
She mused a little, and then clapt her hands
7

'59. Then her false voice made way broken with sobs.
    '*O crueller than was ever told in tale,*
    Or sung in song! O vainly lavish'd love!
    O cruel, there was nothing wild or strange,
    Or seeming shameful, for what shame in *love*,
    So love be true, and not as yours is—nothing
    Poor *Vivien* had not done to *win his trust*
    Who call'd her what he call'd her—all her crime,
    All—all—the wish to prove him wholly hers.'
    She mused a little, and then clapt her hands
                                 (216, 6.)

K. The master-wish to prove him wholly hers.
MS. The wish to prove him wholly *wholly* hers.
'57. The *master*-wish to prove him wholly hers.
'59. *All—all—*the wish to prove him wholly hers.

'57. 'Stabb'd through the *best* affections to the heart!
'59. 'Stabb'd through the *heart's* affections to the heart!
                                     (216, 17.)

'57.   She paused, she hung her head, she wept afresh;
    And the dark wood grew darker toward the storm
    In silence, *and he look'd, and in him died*
    His anger, and he half believed her true,
    Pitied the heaving shoulder and the face,
    Hand-hidden, as for utmost grief or shame,
'59.   She paused, *she turn'd away*, she hung her head,
    The snake of gold slid from her hair, the braid
    Slipt and uncoil'd itself, she wept afresh,
    And the dark wood grew darker toward the storm
    In silence, *while his anger slowly died*
    Within him, till he let his wisdom go
    For ease of heart, and half believed her true:
    Call'd her to shelter in the hollow oak,
    '*Come from the storm' and having no reply,*

THE BEGINNINGS OF THE IDYLLS.   99

  Gazed at the heaving shoulder, and the face
  Hand-hidden, as for utmost grief or shame;
              (217, 11.)

'57. The seeming-*guileless* simple-hearted thing
'59. The seeming-*injured* simple-hearted thing (217, 26.)

'57. *Around her waist in pity, not* in love,
'59. *About her, more in kindness than* in love, (218, 5.)

'57. *I cannot grant you aught* which your gross heart
  Would reckon worth *acceptance.* I will go.
  In truth, but one thing now could make me stay;
  That proof of trust so often *justly* ask'd,
  How justly after that vile *name* of yours
'59. *What should be granted* which your *own* gross heart
  Would reckon worth *the taking?* I will go.
  In truth, but one thing now—*better have died
  Thrice than have ask'd it once*—could make me stay—
  That proof of trust—so often ask'd *in vain!*
  How justly, after that vile *term* of yours, (218, 16.)

'57. My fate or fault, *omitting* gayer youth
'73. My fate or folly, *passing* gayer youth (218, 25.)

'57. *She scarce had* ceased, when out of heaven a bolt
'59. *Scarce had she* ceased, when out of heaven a bolt
              (209, 7.)

'57.   she call'd him lord and liege,
  Her seer, her *sage,* her silver star of eve,
'59.   she call'd him lord and liege,
  Her seer, her *bard,* her silver star of eve, (219, 26.)

(A few minor variations are given in the Appendix.)

5. A Discussion of the Variations in the Text.

A list of all the differences between the early copies of "Enid" and "Nimuë" and the same poems as given in the latest edition of the "Idylls of the King" shows some hundreds of changes made. These are typographical, or verbal, or revisions of the mode of expression, or the omission of entire sentences and the addition of new thoughts. A discussion of these changes made by the poet in his work may easily resolve itself into an expression of personal preference, as, for example, "This change is an improvement; that line was better in the original form,"—a species of criticism which illustrates the differences in men's opinions,* whatever other value it may or may not have. An attempt to find the poet's plan in the changes which he has made has, perhaps, the least possible amount of this element of personal preference.

---

* The following quotations illustrate the well-known line of Terence, "Quot homines, tot sententiæ":

"The story of 'Elaine' denuded of the noble language in which it has been clothed by Mr. Tennyson, would scarcely interest our readers."—*Edinburgh Review*, July, 1859.

"Indeed it was hardly possible to add to the simplicity and pathos of the tale ['Elaine'] as it stands in the pages of Sir Thomas Malory."—Gladstone in the *Quarterly Review*, October, 1859.

"Such a conclusion (for we consider this fourth Idyll ['Guinevere'] mainly in the light of the completion of what has gone before, hardly as a separate poem) goes far to make us forget and forgive the insult which we conceive 'Enid' to

Of the later forms of expression adopted by the poet, some were chosen, apparently, because they express the thought with greater accuracy. Others amplify the thought for the sake of clearness, or add to the beauty of a scene. Lines are omitted which make the impression of the whole less pleasing. Other revisions perfect the rhythm. Many changes, seemingly insignificant as to the difference in thought, are those refinements of expression which give that subtle charm of artistic excellence universally ascribed to him who ranks "the first of English poets in making the art of expression a luxury and an ornament." *

Tennyson is distinguished for the accuracy of his references to Nature in particular, and for the accuracy of his thought and words in general. The revised form manifestly expresses in many cases the poet's thought more exactly. The line (p. 70),

and when Geraint
Beheld her there before him in the field,

---

offer to our understanding. . . . We have here [in 'Guinevere'] a noble idea beautifully worked out."—*Blackwood's Magazine*, November, 1859.

" Finished the four Idylls. The first ['Enid'] and third ['Elaine'] could have come only from a great poet. The second ['Vivien'] and fourth ['Guinevere'] do not seem to me so good."—Note in Longfellow's diary, July 20th, 1859, as quoted by Van Dyke, "The Poetry of Tennyson," p. 330.

" For 'Guinevere' is of an almost indescribable grandeur." —Gladstone, *Quarterly Review*, October, 1859.

* *Edinburgh Review*, October, 1881.

is ambiguous. The expression "before him" may be taken as an adverbial element either of place or of time. The line as given in '59 is free from this obscurity. The "gorgeous gown," the "costly-braided" gift, which Enid laid from her limbs in '57, was probably not a "braided" gown at all, but a "costly-broider'd" gown, as it is more accurately described in '59. The change of *unsolder'd* to *unmortised* (p. 95),

> The feet unsolder'd from their ancle-bones,

is a distinct gain in accuracy. The feet are not "solder'd" to the ankle-bones. The oak before which the "wileful Nimuë" lay at Merlin's feet, so hollow huge and old that it look'd a tower of *ruin'd* masonwork, is certainly more accurately described as resembling a tower of *ivied* masonwork. And yet not until the '86 edition was this change made. In the '57 copy Merlin explains to Nimuë that Sir Sagramore, whose torch had been puffed out by an angry gust of wind, became bewildered "among the many-room'd and many-corridor'd complexities of Arthur's palace," and, finding a door he thought his own,

> *crept to* the couch and slept
> A stainless man beside a stainless maid.

But in '59 Sir Sagramore *made for* the couch and slept, a more accurate and certainly a happier expression in that it does not give the impression of stealthiness produced by the "*crept to* the couch" of the '57 copy.

Many of the changes made were doubtless made to improve the metre, as, for example (p. 84),

THE BEGINNINGS OF THE IDYLLS. 103

K. *And if he be dead*, I count you for a fool,
'57. *And be he dead*, I count you for a fool,

Of these revisions which perfect the rhyme two are of interest because—though so apparent and so easily made—they were in fact not made until the later editions of the poem. The line (p. 71),

For I these two years past have won it for thee,

is the same in '57, '59, '62, '69, '73, '75, '84. Not till the '86 edition do we find,

What I these two years past have won for thee.

The omission of the unnecessary *it* in the following line (p. 81), was made in the '73 edition,

And, Enid, you and he, I see it with joy—

Some changes we may assume to have been made for the sake of felicities of expression, as, for example, Geraint's promise to his new mother to come once more with Enid "some golden day," a manuscript correction unfortunately, perhaps, not preferred to the "some gaudy-day" of '59; or Edyrn's statement to Geraint that at Arthur's court he was waiting to be treated like a wolf, "because they knew my doings" (K.), "because I know they knew my deeds" ('57), "because I knew my deeds were known" ('59); or the reply of Geraint to Edyrn's announcement that he has come to summon the bandit Earl to submit to the judgment of the king. Geraint replies,

K. 'Doorm is disbanded by the King of Fears,
    And suffers judgment from the King of Kings.'
'57. 'He *hath* submitted to the King of Kings.'
'59. 'He hears the judgment of the King of Kings.'

One need but read the three forms in succession to approve the change, the lines preceding being in K. and '57,

> bidding him . . scatter all his powers,
> Submitting to the judgment of the King.'

and in '59,

> bidding him . . scatter all his powers,
> Submit, and hear the judgment of the King.'

Inasmuch as in '59 the two lines are so much alike, the point of difference is thereby emphasized, and the revised form is doubtless the happier expression. We may say the same of Vivien's wailing shriek (p. 98),

'57. 'Stabb'd through the *best* affections to the heart!'
'59. 'Stabb'd through the *heart's* affections to the heart!'

and also of her reply to Merlin, who asks if she has no word of loyal praise " For Arthur, blameless king and stainless man,"

'57. *Him?* is he man at all, who knows and winks?
'59. *Man!* is he man at all, who knows and winks?

Other changes are more than verbal felicities. The new word or the new expression calls up a different picture to the mind's eye. In '57 (p. 75) Geraint doubted whether Enid's acceptance of his love might not be due to "filial softness" in her, a less happy expression than the "filial tenderness" of '59, or the "daughter's tenderness" of '73. So also in '57 (p. 72) Enid expressed a determination to work her fingers "to the bone" in the making of a new gown, certainly a less poetic as well as less accurate expression than that of '59, wherein she says, "myself would work eye dim and finger lame" far liefer than so much discredit him. Enid working her fingers "to the bone" in the making of one new gown (and doing this too in "a day or two") is not the poet's happiest conception.

Not only in what the poet changes or adds, but also in what he omits, does he give new beauty to successive editions of the poem. One of Geraint's most unkindest cuts of all in '57 is omitted in '59, the line (p. 83),

Wellnigh as honest as a weeping wife.

Another omission in the completed "Idylls of the King" is the '57 line (p. 90),

And troubled in his heart about the Queen.

The omission of this line in the completed "Idylls of the King" is exceedingly significant in connection with the question as to the growth of the plan of the poem in the poet's mind. This line makes Arthur suspect Guinevere long before the final disclosures and the consequent disruption of the Order of the Table Round. In the poem as we now have it, the King is not "troubled in heart" about the

Queen at all, but merely "vext" at a rumour issued from Vivien in regard to "some corruption crept among his knights." In the '59 "Elaine," which comes after "Vivien," Guinevere "broke into a scornful laugh,"

He never had a glimpse of mine untruth,

"only to-day there gleamed a vague suspicion in his eyes." As yet, however, nothing but a "vague suspicion," a momentary passing cloud of mistrust; for long after this "the clear face of the guileless King" became her bane. And he in his "white blamelessness," whom Guinevere called in her agony of contrition God's "highest creature here," could as he was passing to death speak of the pang but lately come to him,

Too wholly true to dream untruth in thee.

We may be certain that when Tennyson wrote "Enid and Nimuë" he had not yet planned the outline of the poem in detail. It was impossible that this line should remain in the completed "Idylls of the King." For then must the final disclosures have come apace, or else had the "blameless King" been worthy of Vivien's taunt of being one "who sees and winks." This '57 line retained in "Vivien" would have been fatal to the further development of the "Idylls of the King" through the "Holy Grail," "Pelleas and Ettarre," and "The Last Tournament," which were inserted after "Vivien," between "Elaine" and "Guinevere." The King, notwithstanding his "white blamelessness," could not be "troubled in heart about the Queen" at this stage in the course of events without hastening the disclosures,—he who said when the pang of knowledge finally came,

> Yet must I leave thee, woman, to thy shame.
> I hold that man the worst of public foes
> Who either for his own or children's sake,
> To save his blood from scandal, lets the wife
> Whom he knows false, abide and rule the house;
> . . . .
> Worst of the worse were that man he who reigns!

The existence of this line in the '57 copy is, then, a fact of great moment in establishing the growth in the poet's mind of the plan of the poem as a whole. A corroboration of this view from a linguistic stand-point will be given in connection with a discussion of some changes made in the earlier "Idylls of the King" to weld all into a harmonious whole.

Lord Tennyson doubtless had in mind from the outset some general plan of the course of events in the poem, for at the beginning of "Enid" he makes Guinevere miss the hunt because she

> lay late into the morn,
> Lost in sweet dreams, and *dreaming of her love
> For Launcelot.*

And yet Lancelot is not once mentioned in the story of Geraint in the "Mabinogion," the source from which Lord Tennyson drew his material. The poet introduces, therefore, at the outset the suggestion of the sin about which he groups the events of the whole poem. But the line in the '57 "Nimuë,"

> And troubled in his heart about the Queen,

precludes the possibility of a plan already in the poet's mind of a "blameless king," who could say to Guinevere in "Guinevere," coming after "Lancelot and Elaine," "The Holy Grail," "Pelleas and Ettarre," and "The Last Tournament," that he had been

> Too wholly true to dream untruth in thee.

In '59 he was

> Vext at a rumour rife about the Queen.

In '69, in the volume which included the first four Idylls and also "The Holy Grail," "Pelleas and Ettarre," and "The Passing of Arthur," all coming after "Vivien" in the order of events, the line was printed as in '59. But, as may be seen from the list of variations, Lord Tennyson made in '69 few changes in the text of the poems of the first series of the "Idylls of the King." Indeed, aside from changes in the pronouns from the ordinary to the archaic form, from *you* to *ye*, and in the verbs from *has* to *hath*, and a few changes in punctuation presumably made by the compositor, there was not a single change made in the text of "Vivien" in '69. The new poems were simply inserted in accordance with the requirements of the order of events, without any careful study of their harmony with the poems of the first series. In '73, after the publication of "The Last Tournament" (1871) and "Gareth and Lynette" (1872), when, with the exception of "Balin and Balan" (1885), the "Idylls of the King" was complete, Lord Tennyson, now occupied with the poem as a whole, and not with the composition of the separate parts, observed the inconsistency in this line and substituted in place thereof a line which made Arthur, neither "troubled in his heart about the Queen," nor "vext at a rumour rife about the Queen," but merely "vext" at a rumour issued from Vivien

Of some corruption crept among his knights.

And yet the author of the latest commentary * on the "Idylls of the King" in his discussion of the "Time occupied by the Idylls" places this Idyll of "Merlin and Vivien" as far as possible toward the close. " If the suggested placing of the Idylls is correct, the sin of Lancelot and Guinevere comes much later than at first we are apt to suppose ; this removes some repulsiveness from their guilt and *averts from Arthur the charge of obtuse credulity.*" If even after the omission of this line, "And troubled in his heart about the Queen," the faultless King, that passionate perfection,

Rapt in this fancy of his Table Round,

still needs a defence against the charge of "obtuse

---

* Maccallum, " Tennyson's Idylls of the King and Arthurian Story," p. 427. Macmillan & Co., New York, 1894.

credulity," how hopeless his case would have been, had the line been retained.

In this connection it may be of interest to note the contention* of Kuno Fischer that the plan and the fundamental idea of Goethe's "Faust" were changed during the sixty years of its composition; and not only so, but that the two different fundamental ideas were never harmonized into artistic unity, but remain in the poem to this day,—the unity of the poem, which mirrors the inner life of Goethe himself, lying in the character and the growth of the poet, and being, therefore, more vital, original, and comprehensive than any fabricated, *a priori* plan.

In the '74 edition several consecutive pages were added to "Vivien," viz., from the middle of page 182 to the middle of page 188. These pages describe Vivien's relations to the graceless Mark, her entry into Arthur's court, her sowing of one ill hint from ear to ear, and her "attempt" upon "the blameless King." In the '57 copy we find (p. 90),

> At Merlin's feet the wileful Nimuë lay.
> The wileful Nimuë stole from Arthur's court:
> She hated all the knights because she deem'd
> They wink'd and jested when her name was named.

The '59 edition is like the '57 copy except that *wileful* is changed to *wily* and *Nimuë* to *Vivien*. Not till the '74 edition do we have the six pages referred to

---

* Kuno Fischer, "Goethes Faust, Entstehung, Idee, und Composition," vol. ii. pp. 137–260. Stuttgart, 1893.

THE BEGINNINGS OF THE IDYLLS. 111

above inserted between the first and the second lines of the '57 copy quoted above. The first and second lines of the new matter in the '74 edition have since been changed. In '74 they read,

> Whence came she? One that bare in bitter grudge
> The scorn of Arthur and his Table, Mark

They now read,

> For he that always bare in bitter grudge
> The slights of Arthur and his Table, Mark

A part of this '74 addition to "Vivien" is the minstrel's song,

> That out of naked knightlike purity
> Sir Lancelot worshipt no unmarried girl
> But the great Queen herself, fought in her name,
> Sware by her—vows like theirs, that high in heaven
> Love most, but neither marry, nor are given
> In marriage, angels of our Lord's report.

And inasmuch as this fair example was truly followed by some "so passionate for an utter purity beyond the limit of their bond," "brave hearts and clean!" this picture of the ideal of the Order of the Table Round is in effective contrast with "the maxims of the mud" of Mark's court.

Seven lines describing Merlin's great melancholy (p. 93) were given first in the '73 edition. These lines we should miss greatly from the poem. In them we have a hint of the course of events, of the war between the flesh and the life, of the meanest having power upon the highest, of the doom about to fall, and the high purpose of Arthur in the founding of the Table Round to serve a model for the mighty world, to break the heathen and uphold the Christ and be the fair beginning of a time,—all broken* by the worm of lust.

These lines, resembling those lines in Shakespeare which foreshadow the final catastrophe, inevitable as fate, "What's done, cannot be undone," were added in '73, by which time the "Idylls of the King" was mainly completed. They are an excellent example of the invaluable additions made in successive editions of this great poem, through which, because of its legendary origin, speaks the voice of the race, a poem worthy of philosophical and philological study because of its content and its growth.

---

* Dr. Albert Hamann, Oberlehrer an der Luisenschule, Berlin, Honorary M.A. Oxford, compares the close of the "Idylls of the King" to the Fall of Walhalla in Wagner's "Götterdämmerung." To the poet's Cambridge friend, the Dean of Canterbury, the closing impression does not seem so hopeless. "Thus we have seen the arising and crowning of man's higher soul, and the brightness of its opening reign: then gather round it the storms of passion, of lust, of vain superstition, ever thickening and blasting all fair prospect; until, baffled and discomfited in its earthly hopes, it sinks in the mist of death, but at eventide there is light, and the end is glory."

CHAPTER III.

THE COMPLETED IDYLLS OF THE KING.

1. The "Idylls of the King" as an Organic Unity.

THE topic has been largely discussed whether the "Idylls of the King" is in reality a single poem, an organic unity, or whether it is a series of twelve separate but connected poems which are a succession of panel pictures rather than one magnificent painting. This discussion was doubtless furthered by the fragmentary mode of composition and publication of the poem.

It is true that in the introductory dialogue of the "Morte d'Arthur" of 1842 we have the term epic applied to the hypothetical poem, which had been cast into the fire,—

'You know,' said Frank, 'he burnt
His epic, his King Arthur, some twelve books,'—

but the poet gave no hint in the "Idylls of the King" of 1859 that the four poems then given were intended as parts of a whole. Indeed, the perhaps unduly modest title Idylls seemed to preclude such a view. Yet there were those who appreciated the possibilities of the subject and who looked for a continuation of the Idylls. It was with the prospect of an Arthurian epic in mind that Gladstone wrote in 1859, in his review of this first series of the "Idylls of the King," "We have a cheerful hope that, if he continues to advance upon himself as he has advanced heretofore, nay, if he can keep the level he has gained, such a work will be the greatest, and by far the greatest poetical creation, that, whether in our own or in foreign poetry, the nineteenth century has produced."

After the publication of "The Holy Grail and other Poems" in 1869, the design of the poet was evident, and critics now began to emphasize the plan of the whole in the discussion of the separate poems, and the necessity for the less agreeable members of the series. "The 'Idylls of the King,'" said R. H. Hutton, "has a grander aim and a larger scope"* than any of Tennyson's previous work. The *Edinburgh Review* (April, 1870) now held, not only that the poem is a whole, but that it is a drama, somewhat unusual in form, but of the highest order, "the great drama which he has told in his own individual fashion, but which is not less a tragedy than "Hamlet" or "Lear," with one great leading interest and plan of action. . . . The more it is studied the more manifest it will be that every part of it has been composed with careful reference to the leading conception, and that those individual portions which throw but broken lights, when taken by themselves, become full of force

---

* *Macmillan's Magazine*, London, December, 1872.

THE COMPLETED IDYLLS OF THE KING. 115

and significance when considered in their relation to the rest. Nothing more grand or perfect exists in modern poetry than the plan of this tragedy."

But, however grand or perfect the plan of the poem may now be, a study of the changes made in subsequent additions to those members published in 1859 reveals an important modification, or at least an enlargement of the original plan. Therefore a list of these changes is hereby given. A small proportion of these changes was required by this growth in the plan of the poem. Many are seemingly of slight consequence. Yet, inasmuch as Lord Tennyson esteemed the revised form an improvement sufficient to justify the change, the list is made complete. Most of the changes were made in the '73 or '74 editions.

2. A List of Variations between the First Editions and the Last Edition of the "Idylls of the King."

DEDICATION.

'62.   And indeed He seems to me
      Scarce other than my *own* ideal knight,
'94.   And indeed He seems to me
      Scarce other than my *king's* ideal knight, (1, 7.)

'62. The shadow of His loss *moved* like eclipse,
'94. The shadow of His loss *drew* like eclipse, (1, 14.)

THE COMING OF ARTHUR.

'69. *Rience*, assail'd him: last a heathen horde,
'94. *Urien*, assail'd him: last a heathen horde, (5, 17.)

'69. His tents beside the forest: *and* he drave
   The heathen, *and he* slew the beast, and fell'd
   The forest, *and let* in the sun,
'94. His tents beside the forest. *Then* he drave
   The heathen; *after,* slew the beast, and fell'd
   The forest, *letting* in the sun, (6, 13.)

'69. Flash'd forth and into war: for most of these
   Made head against him,
'94. Flash'd forth and into war: for most of these,
   Colleaguing with a score of petty kings,
   Made head against him, (13, 21.)

'69. And power on this dead world to make it live."
   And Arthur from the field of battle sent
   Ulfius, and Brastias, and Bedivere,
'94. And power on this dead world to make it live.'
   Thereafter—as he speaks who tells the tale—
   When Arthur reach'd a field-of-battle bright
   With pitch'd pavilions of his foe, the world
   Was all so clear about him, that he saw
   The smallest rock far on the faintest hill,
   And even in high day the morning star.
   So when the King had set his banner broad,
   At once from either side, with trumpet-blast,
   And shouts, and clarions shrilling unto blood,
   The long-lanced battle let their horses run.
   And now the Barons and the kings prevail'd,
   And now the King, as here and there that war
   Went swaying; but the Powers who walk the world
   Made lightnings and great thunders over him,
   And dazed all eyes, till Arthur by main might,
   And mightier of his hands with every blow,
   And leading all his knighthood threw the kings
   Carádos, Urien, Cradlemont of Wales,

Claudias, and Clariance of Northumberland,
The King Brandagoras of Latangor,
With Anguisant of Erin, Morganore,
And Lot of Orkney. Then, before a voice
As dreadful as the shout of one who sees
To one who sins, and deems himself alone
And all the world asleep, they swerved and brake
Flying, and Arthur call'd to stay the brands
That hack'd among the flyers, 'Ho! they yield!'
So like a painted battle the war stood
Silenced, the living quiet as the dead,
And in the heart of Arthur joy was lord.
He laugh'd upon his warrior whom he loved
And honor'd most. ' Thou dost not doubt me King,
So well thine arm hath wrought for me to-day.'
' Sir and my liege,' he cried, ' the fire of God
Descends upon thee in the battle-field:
I know thee for my King!' Whereat the two,
For each had warded either in the fight,
Sware on the field of death a deathless love.
And Arthur said, ' Man's word is God in man:
Let chance what will, I trust thee to the death.'
Then quickly from the foughten field he sent
Ulfius, and Brastias, and Bedivere, (7, 23.)

'69. " A doubtful throne is ice on summer seas—
Ye come from Arthur's court: think ye this king—
So few his knights, however brave they be—
Hath body enow to *beat* his foemen down?"
'94. ' A doubtful throne is ice on summer seas.
Ye come from Arthur's court. Victor *his men*
Report him! Yea, but ye—think ye this king—
So many those that hate him, and so strong,
So few his knights, however brave they be—
Hath body enow to *hold* his foemen down?" (13, 24.

'69. 'Take me,' but turn the blade and *you* shall see,
'94. "Take me," but turn the blade and *ye* shall see, (16, 4.)

'69. As nothing, *and* the king stood out in heaven,
'94. As nothing, *but* the King stood out in heaven, (21, 18.)

'69. Stood round him, and rejoicing in his joy.
  And holy Dubric spread his hands and spake,
'94. Stood round him, and rejoicing in his joy.
  Far shone the fields of May thro' open door,
  The sacred altar blossom'd white with May,
  The Sun of May descended on their King,
  They gazed on all earth's beauty in their Queen,
  Roll'd incense, and there past along the hymns
  A voice as of the waters, while the two
  Sware at the shrine of Christ a deathless love:
  And Arthur said, 'Behold, thy doom is mine.
  Let chance what will, I love thee to the death!'
  To whom the Queen replied with drooping eyes,
  'King and my lord, I love thee to the death!'
  And holy Dubric spread his hands and spake, (22, 9.)

'69. Fulfil the boundless purpose of their king."
  Then at the marriage feast came in from Rome,
  The slowly-fading mistress of the world,
  Great lords, who claim'd *the* tribute as of yore.
'94. Fulfil the boundless purpose of their King!'
  So Dubric said; but when they left the shrine
  Great Lords from Rome before the portal stood,
  In scornful stillness gazing as they past;
  Then while they paced a city all on fire
  With sun and cloth of gold, the trumpets blew,
  And Arthur's knighthood sang before the King:—
   'Blow trumpet, for the world is white with May;
   Blow trumpet, the long night hath roll'd away!

Blow thro' the living world—" Let the King reign."
' Shall Rome or Heathen rule in Arthur's realm?
Flash brand and lance, fall battleaxe upon helm,
Fall battleaxe, and flash brand! Let the King reign.
' Strike for the King and live! his knights have heard
That God hath told the King a secret word.
Fall battleaxe, and flash brand! Let the King reign.
' Blow trumpet! he will lift us from the dust.
Blow trumpet! live the strength and die the lust!
Clang battleaxe, and clash brand! Let the King reign.
' Strike for the King and die! and if thou diest,
The King is King, and ever wills the highest.
Clang battleaxe, and clash brand! Let the King reign.
' Blow, for our Sun is mighty in his May!
Blow, for our Sun is mightier day by day!
Clang battleaxe, and clash brand! Let the King reign.
' The King will follow Christ, and we the King
In whom high God hath breathed a secret thing.
Fall battleaxe, and flash brand! Let the King reign.'
So sang the knighthood, moving to their hall.
There at the banquet those great Lords from Rome,
The slowly-fading mistress of the world,
Strode in, and claim'd their tribute as of yore. (22, 26.)

'69. But Arthur spake, " Behold, for these have sworn
To *fight* my wars, and worship me their king ;
'94. But Arthur spake, ' Behold, for these have sworn
To *wage* my wars, and worship me their King ; (24, 11.)

GARETH AND LYNETTE.

'72. ' Lord, we have heard from our wise men at home
'94. Lord, we have heard from our wise man at home
(33, 15.)
'72. But *an* thou wilt no goodlier, then must Kay,
'94. But *so* thou wilt no goodlier, then must Kay, (43, 21.)

'72. Then *while* he donn'd the helm, and took the shield
'94. Then *as* he donn'd the helm, and took the shield
(53, 19.)
'72. The people, *and* from out of kitchen came
'94. The people, *while* from out of kitchen came (53, 23.)

'72. 'Kay, wherefore *will ye* go against the King,
'94. 'Kay, wherefore *wilt thou* go against the King,
(55, 5.)
'72. But *will ye* yield this damsel harbourage?'
'94. But *wilt thou* yield this damsel harbourage?' (59, 16.)

'72. *Ye* be of Arthur's Table,' a light laugh
'94. *You* * be of Arthur's Table,' a light laugh (59, 18.)

'72. 'Friend, whether *ye* be kitchen-knave, or not,
'94. 'Friend, whether *thou* be kitchen-knave, or not,
(61, 6.)
'72. The champion *ye have* brought from Arthur's hall,
'94. The champion *thou hast* brought from Arthur's hall?
(63, 1.)
'72.   And he that bore
    The star, *being* mounted, cried from o'er the bridge,
'94.   And he that bore
    The star, *when* mounted, cried from o'er the bridge,
(64, 12.)
'72. 'Fair damsel, *ye* should worship me the more,
'94. 'Fair damsel, *you* should worship me the more,
(67, 8.)
'72.   'Damsel,' he said, '*ye* be not all to blame,
    Saving that *ye* mistrusted our good King
    Would handle scorn, or yield *thee*, asking, one

---

* Notwithstanding somewhat more than two hundred changes from *you* to *ye*, *have* to *hast*, etc., we have in "Gareth and Lynette" and in "The Last Tournament" some changes from *ye* to *you*.

Not fit to cope *thy* quest. *Ye* said your say;
'94. 'Damsel,' he said, '*you* be not all to blame,
Saving that *you* mistrusted our good King
Would handle scorn, or yield *you*, asking, one
Not fit to cope *your* quest. *You* said your say;
(73, 16.)

'72. To the King's best wish. O damsel, be *ye* wise
'94. To the King's best wish. O damsel, be *you* wise
(77, 6.)

'72. Said Lancelot, 'Peradventure he, *ye* name,
'94. Said Lancelot, 'Peradventure he, *you* name, (78, 22.)

'72. *Ye* cannot scare me; nor rough face, or voice,
'94. *You* cannot scare me; nor rough face, or voice,
(80, 6.)

'72.   At once Sir Lancelot's charger fiercely neigh'd—
At once the black horse bounded forward with him.
'94. At once Sir Lancelot's charger fiercely neigh'd,
✓   *And Death's dark war-horse* bounded forward with
him. (83, 4.)

(The variations in the text of "The Marriage of Geraint" and "Geraint and Enid" are given in chapter ii.)

BALIN AND BALAN.

'85. A goblet on the board by Balin, boss'd
With holy Joseph's legend, on his right
Stood, all of massiest bronze: one side had sea
And ship and sail and angels blowing on it:
And one was rough with *pole and scaffoldage*
Of that low church he built at Glastonbury.

The last two lines in '94 are,

And one was rough with *wattling, and the walls*
Of that low church he built at Glastonbury. (171, 19.)

(The variations in the text of "Merlin and Vivien" are given in chapter ii.)

LANCELOT AND ELAINE.*

'59. For Arthur *when none knew from whence he came,*
Long *ere the people chose him for their k*ing,
Roving the trackless realms of Lyonnesse,
'94. For Arthur, long *before they crown'd him* King,
Roving the trackless realms of Lyonnesse, (222, 15.)

'59. And *one of these, the* king, had on a crown
'94. And *he, that once was* king, had on a crown (223, 1.)

'59. Thither he made and *wound* the gateway horn.
'94. Thither he made, and *blew* the gateway horn. (227, 25.)

'59. And in the four *wild* battles by the shore
'94. And in the four *loud* battles by the shore (232, 18.)

'59. Paused *in* the gateway, standing *by* the shield
'94. Paused *by* the gateway, standing *near* the shield
(236, 18.)

'59. 'How then? who then?' a fury seized *on them,*
'94. 'How then? who then?' a fury seized *them all,*
(239, 22.)

'59. Back to the barrier; then the *heralds* blew
'94. Back to the barrier; then the *trumpets* blew (240, 21.)

---

* In "Lancelot and Elaine" there have been some forty-one changes from *you* to *ye, has* to *hath*, etc. These are,—page and line of the Macmillan edition,—(224, 12, 13, 15); (225, 5, 10, 11, 12); (226, 16); (227, 11); (228, 22); (229, 4, 5); (230, 3, 8, 9); (240, 25); (242, 20); (243, 12, 23); (244, 12, 12); (245, 2); (247, 23. 24); (249, 8, 9); (250, 22); (251, 9, 12); (256, 24); (261, 19, 21, 22); (262, 1, 18, 20); (264, 18); (272, 13); (273, 5); 275, 23).

'59. Draw'—and Lavaine drew, and *that other* gave
  A marvellous great shriek and ghastly groan,
'94. Draw,'—and Lavaine drew, and *Sir Lancelot* gave
  A marvellous great shriek and ghastly groan,
            (241, 12.)
'59. He must not pass uncared for. *Gawain*, rise,
  My nephew, and ride forth and find the knight.
'94. He must not pass uncared for. *Wherefore*, rise,
  O Gawain, and ride forth and find the knight. (242, 8.)

'59.   *Wherefore* take
  This diamond, and deliver it, and return,
  And bring us *what* he is and how he fares,
'94.   *Rise and* take
  This diamond, and deliver it, and return,
  And bring us *where* he is, and how he fares, (247, 17.)

'59. And *Lamorack*, a good knight, but therewithal
  Sir Modred's brother, *of a crafty house*,
'94. And *Gareth*, a good knight, but therewithal
  Sir Modred's brother, *and the child of Lot*, (243, 4.)

'59. Ill news, my Queen, for all who love him, *these!*
'94. Ill news, my Queen, for all who love him, *this!*—
            (244, 18.)

'59. *Moved* to her chamber, and there flung herself
'94. *Past* to her chamber, and there flung herself (245, 4.)

'59. The victor, but had *ridden wildly* round
'94. The victor, but had *ridd'n a random* round (245, 25.)

'59. And ride no *longer wildly*, noble Prince!
'94. And ride no *more at random*, noble Prince! (246, 3.)

'59. Who lost the hern we slipt *him* at, and went
'94. Who lost the hern we slipt *her* at, and went (247, 1.)

'59. *Methinks* there is none other I can love.'
'94. *I know* there is none other I can love.' (247, 21.)

'59. *May it be so?* why then, far be it from me
'94. *Nay—like enow:* why then, far be it from me (248, 4.)

'59. Marr'd her friend's *point* with pale tranquillity.
'94. Marr'd her friend's *aim* with pale tranquillity. (249, 25.)

'59. And when they gain'd the cell *in which* he slept,
'94. And when they gain'd the cell *wherein* he slept,
(252, 26.)

'59. And past beneath the *wildly*-sculptured gates
'94. And past beneath the *wierdly*-sculptured gates (254, 5.)

'59. Full often the *sweet* image of one face,
'94. Full often the *bright* image of one face, (255, 16.)

'59. Seeing I *must* go to-day:' then out she brake;
'94. Seeing I go to-day:' then out she brake: (257, 8.)

'59. To *which* the gentle sister made reply,
'94. To *whom* the gentle sister made reply, (263, 4.)

'59. *Steer'd* by the dumb went upward with the flood—
'94. *Oar'd* by the dumb, went upward with the flood—
(266, 10.)

'59. The shadow of *a* piece of pointed lace,
'94. The shadow of *some* piece of pointed lace, (267, 4.)

✓ '59. Then while Sir Lancelot leant, in half *disgust*
'94. Then while Sir Lancelot leant, in half *disdain* (269, 16.)

'59. But Arthur who beheld his cloudy brows
    Approach'd him, and with full affection *flung*
    One *arm about his neck, and spake and* said.
      'Lancelot, my Lancelot, thou in whom I have
    Most *love* and most alliance,

'94. But Arthur, who beheld his cloudy brows,
Approach'd him, and with full affection said,
 'Lancelot, my Lancelot, thou in whom I have
 Most *joy* and most affiance,   (274, 8.)

'59.   but now I would to God,
 For the wild people say wild things of thee,
 Thou could'st have loved this maiden,
'94.   but now I would to God,
 Seeing the homeless trouble in thine eyes,
 Thou couldst have loved this maiden, (274, 17.)

'59. Lancelot, whom the Lady of the *l*ake
 Stole from his mother—*as the story runs*—
 She chanted snatches of mysterious *song*
'94. Lancelot, whom the Lady of the *L*ake
 Caught from his mother's *arms—the wondrous one*
 Who passes thro' the vision of the night—
 She chanted snatches of mysterious *hymns* (276, 9.)

THE HOLY GRAIL.

'69. O *then*, perchance, when all our wars are done,
 The brand Excalibur will be cast away.
'94. O *there*, perchance, when all our wars are done,
 The brand Excalibur will be cast away. (288, 14.)

'69. But *you*, that follow but the leader's bell,'
'94. But *ye*, that follow but the leader's bell" (290, 11.)

'69. *The* chance of noble deeds will come and go
 Unchallenged, while *you* follow wandering fires
'94. *This* chance of noble deeds will come and go
 Unchallenged, while *ye* follow wandering fires (291, 7.)

'69. Before *you* leave him for this *q*uest, may count
'94. Before *ye* leave him for this *Q*uest, may count (291, 14.)

'69. Calling 'God speed!' but in the *street* below
'94. Calling "God speed!" but in the *ways* below (292, 15.)

'69. For *sorrow*, and *in the* middle street the queen,
'94. For *grief*, and *all in* middle street the Queen, (292, 19.)

'69.   and I was left alone
    And *wearied* in a land of sand and thorns.
    "And *on I rode* and found a mighty hill,
'94.   and I was left alone
    And *wearying* in a land of sand and thorns.
    'And *I rode on* and found a mighty hill, (295, 6.)

'69. 'That so cried upon me?' and he had
'94. "That so cried *out* upon me?" and he had (295, 20.)

'69. "*Then* rose a hill that none but man could climb,
'94. '*There* rose a hill that none but man could climb,
                                                     (297, 24.)

'69. *Whither* I made, and there was I disarmed
'94. *Thither* I made, and there was I disarm'd (301, 6.)

'69. For Lancelot's kith and kin *adore him so*
'94. For Lancelot's kith and kin *so worship him* (304, 5.)

PELLEAS AND ETTARRE.

'69. Which? tell us quickly."
                     And Palleas gazing thought,
   "Is Guinevere herself so beautiful?"
'94. Which? tell us quickly.'
                   Palleas gazing thought,
   'Is Guinevere herself so beautiful?' (317, 21.)

'69. "Ay," thought Gawain, "and *ye* be fair enow:
'94. 'Ay,' thought Gawain, 'and *you* be fair enow: (331, 1.)

THE COMPLETED IDYLLS OF THE KING. 127

'69. *The night was hot:* he could not rest, but rode
Ere midnight to her walls,
'94. *Hot was the night and silent; but a sound*
Of Gawain ever coming, and this lay—
Which Pelleas had heard sung before the Queen,
And seen her sadden listening—vext his heart,
And marr'd his rest—' A worm within the rose.'
   ' A rose, but one, none other rose had I,
A rose, one rose, and this was wondrous fair,
One rose, a rose that gladden'd earth and sky,
One rose, my rose, that sweeten'd all mine air—
I cared not for the thorns; the thorns were there.
   ' One rose, a rose to gather by and by,
One rose, a rose, to gather and to wear,
No rose but one—what other rose had I?
One rose, my rose; a rose that will not die,—
He dies who loves it,—if the worm be there.'
   This tender rhyme, and evermore the doubt,
' Why lingers Gawain with his golden news?'
So shook him that he could not rest, but rode
Ere midnight to her walls,
                                                (331, 8.)

'69.   Then he crost the court,
And saw the postern portal also wide
Yawning; and up a slope of garden, all
Of roses white and red, and *white ones* mixt
And overgrowing them, went on, and found,
'94.   Then he crost the court,
And spied not any light in hall or bower,
But saw the postern portal also wide
Yawning; and up a slope of garden, all
Of roses white and red, and *brambles* mixt
And overgrowing them, went on, and found,
                                                (332, 9.)

'69. Then was he ware *that white* pavilions *rose,*
Three from the bushes, gilden-peakt:
'94. Then was he ware *of three* pavilions *rear'd
Above* the bushes, gilden-peakt: (332, 18.)

'69.   O towers so strong,
So solid, would that even while I gaze
'94.   O towers so strong,
Huge, solid, would that even while I gaze (334, 3.)

'69. "*I have* no name," he shouted, a "a scourge am I,
'94. '*No name,* no name,' he shouted, 'a scourge am I
(338, 5.)
'69. "Fight therefore," yelled the *other,* and either knight
'94. 'Fight therefore,' yelled the *youth,* and either knight
(338, 12.)

THE LAST TOURNAMENT.

'71. 'Would rather *ye* had let them fall,' she cried,
'94. 'Would rather *you* had let them fall,' she cried,
(341, 19.)
'71. But under her black brows a swarthy *dame*
'72. But under her black brows a swarthy *one* (348, 22.)

'71. Come—let us *comfort* their sad eyes, our Queen's
'72. Come—let us *gladden* their sad hearts, our Queen's
(349, 5.)
'71. *Then* being ask'd, 'Why skipt ye not, Sir Fool?'
'94. *And* being ask'd, 'Why skipt ye not, Sir Fool?'
(350, 14.)
'71. Than any broken music *ye can* make.'
'94. Than any broken music *thou canst* make.' (350, 17.)

'71. Head-heavy, *while* the knights, who watch'd him,
      roar'd
'94. Head-heavy; *then* the knights, who watch'd him,
      roar'd   (359, 2.)

'71. Then, *yell with yell echoing,* they fired the tower,
'94. Then, *echoing yell with yell,* they fired the tower,
(359, 12.)
'71. What, *an* she hate me now? I would not this.
What *an* she love me still? I would not that.
'94. What, *if* she hate me now? I would not this.
What, *if* she love me still? I would not that.
(360, 5.)
'71. The greater man, the greater courtesy.
But thou, thro' ever harrying thy wild beasts—
'94. The greater man, the greater courtesy.
✓ *Far other was the Tristram, Arthur's knight!*
But thou, thro' ever harrying thy wild beasts—
(365, 16.)
'71. 'Vows! did *ye* keep the vow *ye* made to Mark
'94. 'Vows! did *you* keep the vow *you* made to Mark
(366, 15.)
'71. Bind me to one? The *great* world laughs at it.
'72. Bind me to one? The *wide* world laughs at it.
(368, 1.)
'71.   He rose, he turn'd, *and* flinging round her neck,
Claspt it; *but while he bow'd himself to lay*
Warm kisses in the hollow of her throat,
Out of the dark, just as the lips had touch'd,
Behind him rose a shadow and a shriek—
'Mark's way,' said Mark, and clove him thro' the brain.
'72.   He rose, he turn'd, *then,* flinging round her neck,
✓ Claspt it, *and cried ' Thine Order, O my Queen!'*
But, while he bow'd to kiss the jewell'd throat,
Out of the dark, just as the lips had touch'd,
Behind him rose a shadow and a shriek—
'Mark's way,' said Mark, and clove him thro' the brain. (370, 6.)

GUINEVERE.

'59. For hither had she fled, her cause of flight
Sir Modred; he *nearest to the King,*
His nephew, ever like a subtle beast
Lay couchant with his eyes upon the throne,
'94. For hither had she fled, her cause of flight
Sir Modred; he *that* like a subtle beast
Lay couchant with his eyes upon the throne, (371, 9.)

'59. And then they were agreed upon a night
(When the good King should not be there) to meet
And part for ever. Passion-pale they met
'94. And then they were agreed upon a night
(When the good King should not be there) to meet
✓   And part for ever. *Vivien, lurking, heard.*
She told Sir Modred. Passion-pale they met (374, 26.)

'59. They found a naked child upon the sands
Of wild *Dundagil* by the Cornish sea;
'94. They found a naked child upon the sands
Of dark *Tintagil* by the Cornish sea; (382, 20.)

'59. Came to that point, *when* first she saw the King
'94. Came to that point *where* first she saw the King
(387, 5.)

'59. To speak no slander, no, nor listen to it,
To lead sweet lives in purest chastity,
'94. To speak no slander, no, nor listen to it,
✓   ↲ *To honour his own word as if his God's,*
To lead sweet lives in purest chastity, (389, 22.)

'59. And all this throve *until* I wedded thee!
✓ '94. And all this throve *before* I wedded thee, (390, 8.)

'59. They summon me their King to lead mine hosts
Far down to that great battle in the west,

Where I must strike against my sister's son,
Leagued with *the lords* of the White Horse and knights
Once mine, and strike him dead, and meet myself
Death, or I know not what mysterious doom.
'94. They summon me their King to lead mine hosts
Far down to that great battle in the west,
Where I must strike against *the man they call*
My sister's son—*no kin of mine, who leagues*
With *L*ords of the White Horse, *heathen*, and knights,
Traitors—and strike him dead, and meet myself
Death, or I know not what mysterious doom. (393, 16.)

'59. I thought I could not breathe in that fine air
That pure severity of perfect light—
I *wanted* warmth and colour which I found
In Lancelot—
'94. I thought I could not breathe in that fine air
That pure severity of perfect light—
I *yearn'd* * warmth and colour which I found
In Lancelot— (396, 14.)

THE PASSING OF ARTHUR.

'69. With whom he dwelt, new faces, other minds.
Before that last weird battle in the *West*
'94. With whom he dwelt, new faces, other minds.
For on their march to westward, Bedivere,
Who slowly paced among the slumbering host,
Heard in his tent the moanings of the King:
  ' I found Him in the shining of the stars,
I mark'd Him in the flowering of His fields,
But in His ways with men I find Him not.
I waged His wars, and now I pass and die.
O me! for why is all around us here

---

* A misprint for *yearn'd for* found in other editions.

*As if some lesser god had made the world,
But had not force to shape it as he would,
Till the High God behold it from beyond,
And enter it, and make it beautiful?
Or else as if the world were wholly fair,
But that these eyes of men are dense and dim,
And have not power to see it as it is:
Perchance, because we see not to the close;—
For I, being simple, thought to work His will,
And have but stricken with the sword in vain;
And all whereon I lean'd in wife and friend
Is traitor to my peace, and all my realm
Reels back into the beast, and is no more.
My God, thou hast forgotten me in my death:
Nay—God my Christ—I pass but shall not die.'
   Then, ere that last weird battle in the west,*

(399, 5.)

'69. Once thine, whom thou hast loved, but *baser now*
    Than heathen *scoffing* at their vows and thee.
'94. Once thine, whom thou hast loved, but *grosser grown*
    Than heathen, *spitting* at their vows and thee.

(401, 18.)

'69. " Far other is this battle in the *W*est
    Whereto we move, than when we strove in youth
    *An*d thrust the heathen from the Roman wall,
    And shook him thro' the north.
'94. ' Far other is this battle in the *w*est
    Whereto we move, than when we strove in youth
    *An*d brake the petty kings, and fought with Rome,
    Or thrust the heathen from the Roman wall,
    And shook him thro' the north. (401, 22.)

'69. And the long mountain ended in a coast
'94. And the long mountain*s* ended in a coast (402, 17.)

'69.   only the *waste* wave
   Brake in among dead faces,
'94.   only the *wan* wave
   Brake in among dead faces, (404, 10.)

'69. And dropping bitter tears against *his* brow
   Striped with dark blood:
'94. And dropping bitter tears against *a* brow
   Striped with dark blood: (414, 15.)

'69. And on the mere the wailing died away.
   At length he groan'd, and turning slowly clomb
   The last hard footstep of that iron crag;
'94. And on the mere the wailing died away.
   But when that moan had past for evermore,
✓ *The stillness of the dead world's winter dawn*
   Amazed him, and he groan'd, ' The King is gone.'
   And therewithal came on him the weird rhyme,
   ' From the great deep to the great deep he goes.'
   Whereat he slowly turn'd and slowly clomb
   The last hard footstep of that iron crag; (416, 26.)

'69. *E'en* to the highest he could climb, and saw,
'94. *Ev'n* to the highest he could climb, and saw, (417, 22.)

3. The Growth in the Plan of the Poem as indicated by the Changes made in the Language.

Assuming that the "Idylls of the King" is a single poem, an organic unity, and therefore to be ranked with the "In Memoriam" as one of the two great works upon which the poet's fame will ultimately rest as being not only a singer of exquisite lyrics but also a maker of great poems, it may yet be questioned how clearly the poet had the plan of the whole in mind when he published the first poems of the series. The changes made in these poems, aside from their bearing upon the development of the poet's literary art, have an importance from the light thereby thrown upon the growth of the plan of the poem in the poet's mind.

A frequently recurring change made in the poems of the first series of the "Idylls of the King" is the change of the pronouns and the verbs connected therewith from the ordinary to the archaic form,—from *you* to *ye, your* to *thy,* have to *hast, does* to *doth,* etc. The list following shows the date when these changes were made in the two poems of the '57 copy. It will be noticed that this change to the archaic form began even in the first ('59) edition. Many of the changes were made in the '69 edition. The poet made the changes in the latter portion of "Enid" in '69 (with two exceptions), leaving the first portion largely untouched until '73. In "Vivien" also the changes were made mainly in the '73 edition.

CHANGES IN PRONOUNS AND VERBS FROM THE ORDINARY TO THE ARCHAIC FORM.

"Enid."

PAGE.	LINE.	'57.	'69.	'73.
90	7	you	...	thou
...	7	your	...	thy
95	24	You [Ye '59]	...	......
96	2	you	ye	......
...	26	you	ye	......
99	7	you	...	ye

THE COMPLETED IDYLLS OF THE KING. 135

PAGE.	LINE.	'57.	'69.	'73.
101	19	you	ye	......
102	2	you	...	ye
103	24	your	...	thine
...	24	yours	...	thine
104	13	you	...	thou
...	13	have	...	hast
...	13	can	...	canst
...	15	Your	...	Thy
111	25	you	ye	......
112	14	you	...	ye
113	8	you	ye	......
...	15	you	ye	......
115	18	your	...	thy
120	2	you	...	ye
...	4	you	...	thee
...	4	your	...	thy
122	16	you	...	ye
...	16	you	...	ye
125	3	You	Ye	......
...	7	you	ye	......
127	21	you	...	thou
128	10	You	Ye	......
...	17	you	...	thou
...	17	are	...	art
...	19	you	...	thee
...	20	you	...	ye
129	25	you	ye	......
131	13	does	...	doth
...	20	has	...	hath
...	22	You	...	Ye
132	7	You	...	Ye
...	9	does	...	doth
...	18	you	...	ye

PAGE.	LINE.	'57.	'69.	'73.
...	24	no	...	nay
...	25	you	...	ye
133	7	you	...	thee
135	17	Your [Thy '59]	...	......
...	21	You	Ye	......
...	24	you	ye	......
...	26	you	ye	......
136	8	you	ye	......
137	4	You	Ye	......
138	21	you	ye	......
...	24	you	ye	......
141	5	you	ye	......
...	5	you	ye	......
...	8	You	Ye	......
...	13	you [ye '59]	...	......
144	7	you	...	ye
146	4	you	ye	......
146	10	you	ye	......
...	15	you	ye	......
151	14	you	ye	......
...	19	you	ye	......
154	15	you	ye	......
...	23	you	ye	......
...	24	you	ye	......
155	3	does	...	doth

"Nimuë" ("Vivien").

191	21	you	ye	......
...	22	you	ye	......
...	23	you	ye	......
193	2	you	...	ye
...	20	yes	...	ay
...	21	you	...	ye
...	24	you	...	ye

THE COMPLETED IDYLLS OF THE KING. 137

PAGE.	LINE.	'57.	'69.	'73.
194	22	you	ye	......
...	23	you	ye	......
195	7	you	...	ye
...	17	you	...	ye
196	9	you	ye	......
...	14	you	ye	......
197	3	you	...	ye
...	11	you	...	ye
198	4	you	ye	......
199	25	you	ye	......
200	21	you	...	ye
...	23	you	...	ye
201	19	you	...	ye
...	19	you	...	ye
202	20	you	...	ye
...	20	you	...	ye
203	2	you	...	ye
...	2	you	...	ye
...	19	you	...	ye
204	1	you	...	ye
...	5	you	ye	......
206	2	Your	...	Thy
...	2	yourself	...	thyself
208	1	you	...	ye
...	16	You	...	Thou
...	25	you	...	thou
209	12	you	...	ye
...	12	swore	...	sware
...	12	you	...	ye
...	14	you	...	ye
210	1	you	...	ye
...	2	you	...	ye
211	1	are	...	art

PAGE.	LINE.	'57.	'69.	'73.
...	1	you	...	thou
212	22	you	...	ye
213	4	you	...	ye
218	22	has	...	hath
219	1	you	...	thee
...	2	you	...	thee
...	3	your	...	thy

In comparison with the later members of the poem the first four members as originally published are in their literary form and language stories of the past told in the language of the present. The changes to the archaic form of speech throw a different coloring over the whole. We feel in the later members of the series a different poetical atmosphere. Not only are the stories told stories of the past, but the language also becomes the language of the past. The very form of speech carries us back in spirit to that mythical time when King Arthur with his mystic sword, Excalibur, that rose from out the bosom of the lake, "drave" the heathen out, and after slew the beast, and fell'd the forest, letting in the sun. And heeding then the call of his brother king, Leodogran, on whom the heathen horde "brake,"

> Reddening the sun with smoke and earth with blood,
> And on the spike that split the mother's heart
> Spitting the child,

he arose and came. And before his voice they swerved and "brake" flying. And then he felt the light of Guinevere's eyes into his life smite on the sudden and he felt travail, and throes and agonies of the life, desiring to be joined with Guinevere, until they "sware" at the shrine of Christ a deathless love and had power on the dark land to lighten it. Then, relying upon the puissance of his Table Round, Arthur "spake" at the marriage banquet denying the tribute to the great Lords of Rome. And Arthur strove with Rome, and made a realm and reigned.

It is true that these archaic forms of speech are not entirely wanting in the poems of the first series. We find even in the '57 copy an occasional *spake* and *brake* and *drave* and *clave*, though the ordinary forms predominate. But in the later poems the archaic forms predominate. Indeed, there is not a single use of the form "spoke" in the "Coming of Arthur," though "spake" occurs many times.

In the "Morte d'Arthur" of 1842 we have in nearly every case the archaic form of the pronouns and the verbs. In the '59 edition we have as uniformly the ordinary forms. These were later changed to the archaic forms. If in '59 the poet had a definite plan of connecting these poems with the "Morte d'Arthur" into an epic of King Arthur, then the query suggests itself why he did not in the first edition of these poems use these archaic forms which he had already employed in the "Morte d'Arthur," which he used in the later members of the poem, and to which in some two hundred instances the verbs and pronouns of the first series were changed in the second or the third edition of these poems.

To Stopford A. Brooke, with the introduction of the allegory into the poem in 1869, "the inner intention of the whole poem seems to be changed." It was perhaps with this introduction of the allegory that the change to the archaic language was determined upon in order to heighten the effect of the allegory by removing "some modern touches here and there" in the language. This use of archaic language supports the symbolism in transforming him who had been the resplendent top of human excellence, "a modern gentleman of stateliest port," into a type as well, a type of the Conscience, of the higher soul of man.

4. The Growth in the Plan of the Poem as indicated by the Changes made in Consequence of the Introduction of the Allegory.

In the epilogue "To the Queen" occur the lines,

. . . But thou, my Queen,
. . . accept this old imperfect tale,
New-old, and shadowing Sense at war with Soul
Rather than that old gray king, whose name, a ghost,
Streams like a cloud, man-shaped, from moutain peak
And cleaves to cairn and cromlech still;

In the first series of this poem there was nothing of this "shadowing Sense at war with Soul." The king, who becomes to some extent "a ghost" in the later poems, a type* of the "higher soul of man,"

---

* "Now this higher soul of man, in its purity, in its justice, in its nobleness, in its self-denial, we understand Mr. Tenny-

"the Conscience," "the innate moral sense," appeared in none of these aspects in the early poems. And in none of the early reviews was he taken as "figuring forth" the Conscience or any other of the moral virtues. In *Blackwood's Magazine* (November, 1859) we read, "Lancelot is the favorite of the old romances; Mr. Tennyson makes him a more noble-minded man than they do, and yet elevates Arthur, the man who endures, immeasurably high above Lancelot, the man who inflicts the injury." Gladstone said, "We know not where to look in history or in letters for a nobler and more overpowering conception of man as he might be than in the Arthur of this volume. Wherever he appears it is as the great pillar of the moral order, and the resplendent top of human excellence."

But since 1869 Sense is manifestly more or less at war with Soul in the poem, though the allegory does not impress all readers with equal prominence. To Andrew Lang the blameless King now becomes almost too obviously allegoric. "It is not so much the fault of the Laureate's genius, as of literary necessity, that the 'Idylls' are almost too obviously

---

son to figure forth by 'the King.'"—The Dean of Canterbury in the *Contemporary Review*, London, January, 1870.

This exposition is of especial value because its author (a life-long friend, one of the Cambridge circle of gifted youth which included Tennyson and Arthur Hallam) is presumably giving the poet's own interpretation of his poem. Dean Alford's words expressly are, "This exposition,—which is not, we beg to say, a mere invention of our own,—"

allegoric. . . . The voice is not the voice of the Arthur whom we knew. The knight has become a type; a type he remains through the cycle of the 'Idylls of the King.' It is not our Arthur who preaches to the penitent Guinevere: the King has become the Conscience."* Professor Dowden has written, "What is the central point in the ethical import of the Arthurian story as told by Mr. Tennyson? It is the assertion that the highest type of manhood is set forth in the poet's ideal King, and that the worthiest work of man is work such as his." † Henry Elsdale, in a work ‡ which was the first elaborate explanation of the allegory in the "Idylls of the King," manifestly regards Arthur as a man with human imperfections no less than as a type of the higher soul of man. Of the farewell at Almesbury he has written, " Instead of declaiming against his poor prostrate wife in the convent, from the vantage-ground of a lofty and irreproachable morality, he should rather have knelt down in the dust beside her and confessed that he himself was partly to blame—that he had never loyally striven to understand her, to meet her just claims, to enter into her wishes, to share her thoughts—in fact, that he had neglected the wife for whose safe custody he was responsible before his God." Others detect in these lofty reproaches a vein of "insuf-

---

* Sommer's " Le Morte Darthur."
† "Studies in Literature," London, 1878.
‡ "Studies in the Idylls," London, 1878.

ferable self-righteousness," not to say "priggishness." He who to one is the voice of the Conscience is to another self-righteous and priggish. To the latter at least the King is not "too obviously allegoric."

Our concern is not, however, with the allegory itself, but with the changes made in the poems of the first series in consequence of the introduction of the allegory.

In 1859, when there was no thought of making the Lady of the Lake symbolical of religion, she was merely one of the fairies whose custom was to "steal babies,"* and she "stole" Lancelot from his mother's arms and chanted snatches of "mysterious songs." But with the change in the conception of the Lady of the Lake in 1869 this description was no longer congruous, and she now "caught" Lancelot from his mother's arms, she

—the wondrous one
Who passes thro' the vision of the night—
She chanted snatches of mysterious *hymns*

Thus by the substitution of two words and the addition of one line the babe-stealing fairy of the

---

* " In all this we recognize the familiar figure of the heroine of many a Celtic tale; she steals babies. . . . The Lady of the Lake had a very distinct object in view in appropriating the child Lancelot. . . . She took him to her own land, consisting of an isle surrounded by impassable walls in the middle of the sea, whence the fairy derived her name of *la Dame du Lac*, or the Lady of the Lake, and her foster-son that of Lancelot du Lac."—J. Rhys, " Studies in the Arthurian Legend," p. 128.

'59 edition becomes the Church in '69, and it may now be fitly said of her in the "Coming of Arthur" that

> She gave the King his huge cross-hilted sword,
> Whereby to drive the heathen out: a mist
> Of incense curl'd about her, and her face
> Wellnigh was hidden in the minster gloom;
> But there was heard among the holy hymns
> A voice as of the waters,

In 1859, Arthur the king was a man and Modred and Gawain were his nephews. It is true that the poet has said that by Arthur he always meant the soul.* However, with the introduction of the allegory into the later poems, the statement of his relationship to Modred and Gawain was omitted. Indeed, an explicit denial of the relationship was introduced. In '59, Arthur, referring to the unknown victor (Lancelot) sore wounded in the diamond joust at Camelot, said,

> He must not pass uncared for. Gawain, rise,
> *My nephew*, and ride forth and find the knight.

These lines now read,

---

* "Of the 'Idylls of the King' he said, 'When I was twenty-four I meant to write a whole great poem on it, and began it in the "Morte d'Arthur." I said I should do it in twenty years; but the Reviews stopped me. . . . By King Arthur I always meant the soul, and by the Round Table the passions and capacities of a man. There is no grander subject in the world than King Arthur.'"—James Knowles, *The Nineteenth Century*, London, January, 1893.

He must not pass uncared for. Wherefore, rise,
O Gawain, and ride forth and find the knight.

In '59, Guinevere had fled to the holy house at Almesbury,

> her cause of flight
> Sir Modred; he nearest to the King,
> *His nephew*, ever like a subtle beast
> Lay couchant with his eyes upon the throne,

lines which now read,

> her cause of flight
> Sir Modred; he that like a subtle beast
> Lay couchant with his eyes upon the throne,

In '59, while Arthur is bidding Guinevere farewell and has expressed the hope that hereafter they two may meet before high God, he hears a trumpet blow and says, Now must I hence,

> They summon me their King to lead mine hosts
> Far down to that great battle in the west,
> Where I must strike against *my sister's son*,

a line which was changed to

> Where I must strike against *the man they call
> My sister's son—no kin of mine*,

In chapter ii. there is a discussion of the significance of the omission of the line,

> And troubled in his heart about the Queen.

A change made in a line of "Lancelot and Elaine" was apparently made with the same purport, viz., to justify the guilelessness of the King in the early portion of the poem by omitting or revising those lines not consistent with the King's declaration to Guinevere near the close of the poem that he had been

Too wholly true to dream untruth in thee.

In '59, Arthur, expressing his regret that Lancelot had not loved the lily maid of Astolat, whose "gorgeous obsequies" had now been celebrated, said to him,

I would to God,
For the wild people say wild things of thee,
Thou couldst have loved this maiden, shaped, it seems
By God for thee alone.

The "wild things" which the "wild people" were saying of Lancelot was, perhaps,

Lo the shameless ones, who take
Their pastime now the trustful King is gone!

By putting in place of the line,

For the wild people say wild things of thee,

the line,

Seeing the homeless trouble in thine eyes,

Arthur is made less liable to the charge of obtuseness in that he is not represented as closing his ears to testimony, but is represented rather as attributing to homelessness the trouble in the eyes of him with whom he, at the close of the great day when the heathen were put to rout and each had warded either in the fight,

> Sware on the field of death a deathless love.
> 'Man's word is God in man;
> Let chance what will, I trust thee to the death.'

After this glorious vow, if such vows be indeed more than the wholesome madness of an hour, who would wish the blameless King to be less guileless, or to sully with suspicion his soul, who would not wish him to rather die than doubt his warrior whom he loved and honored most. *Let chance what will, I trust thee to the death.*

5. The Philological Study of the Poetry of Tennyson.

The "Idylls of the King" resembles Goethe's "Faust," not only in the use of legendary material and in having an allegorical signification, but also in respect to the length of time during which it grew into completeness, and a comparative study of the language and the matter of the earlier and the later portions will doubtless repay the philological investigator with some portion of the rich results already derived from a similar study of "Faust."

Not alone the "Idylls of the King," but also the poetry of Tennyson in general, gives opportunity for such study in consequence of the changes made in successive editions of these poems. And inasmuch as Tennyson is a consummate literary artist, "the first of English poets in making the art of expression a luxury and an ornament," these changes have a value to those who would therefrom study the workings of the poet's mind and discover the method of workmanship and the literary art of him who is "one of the greatest masters of metre, both simple and sonorous, that the English language has ever known."

And not only an appreciation of Tennyson's literary art, but also a knowledge of his final view of life, is acquired by this study. Stopford A. Brooke speaks of "the sceptical trouble of the confused and wavering time during which the 'Idylls' were written. . . . Few then kept their faith, whether in God and Man, or Man alone. . . . And the 'Idylls of the King' represent this wavering between hope and despondency, between faith and unfaith in either God or man."

And this wavering in the poet's view of life could be distinctly traced in his works by determining the order in which the various portions thereof were written. In the earliest 'Idyll,' the "Enid" of the '57 copy, we hear the song of brave-hearted Enid, broken in fortune but not in spirit, the song of Fortune and her wheel,

> Turn, Fortune, turn thy wheel with smile or frown;
> With that wild wheel we go not up or down;
> Our hoard is little, but our hearts are great.
>
> Thy wheel and thee we neither love nor hate,
> . . . .
> For man is man and *master of his fate*.

In the year after the last "Idyll" was published we read in " Locksley Hall Sixty Years After,"

Follow Light, and do the Right—for *man can half-control his doom.*

Though this is not a cry of despair, but rather a brave recognition that the Present is fatal Daughter of the Past, by one who is none the less hopeful that Love will conquer at the last, yet there is not here the exultant Vision of the world and all the wonder that would be of the early poems, nor is there here the serene faith of the work of the poet's old age.

It is, then, not a matter of indifference to the student of Tennyson that the noble passage in " The Passing of Arthur" celebrating the power of prayer was in the "Morte d'Arthur" of the young poet in 1842,

Pray for my soul. More things are wrought by prayer
Than this world dreams of. Wherefore, let thy voice
Rise like a fountain for me night and day.
For what are men better than sheep or goats
That nourish a blind life within the brain,
If, knowing God, they lift not hands of prayer
Both for themselves and those who call them friends?
For so the whole round earth is every way
Bound by gold chains about the feet of God,

and that the following passage with its note of uncertainty appeared somewhat more than thirty years later,

'I found Him in the shining of the stars,
I mark'd Him in the flowering of His fields,
But in His ways with men I find Him not.

I waged His wars, and now I pass and die.
O me! for why is all around us here
As if some lesser god had made the world,
But had not force to shape it as he would,
Till the High God behold it from beyond,
And enter it, and make it beautiful?
Or else as if the world were wholly fair,
But that these eyes of men are dense and dim,
And have not power to see it as it is:
Perchance, because we see not to the close;—
For I, being simple, thought to work His will,
And have but stricken with the sword in vain;
And all whereon I lean'd in wife and friend
Is traitor to my peace, and all my realm
Reels back into the beast, and is no more.
My God, thou hast forgotten me in my death:
Nay—God my Christ—I pass but shall not die.'

This view of life,

> For so the whole round earth is every way
> Bound by gold chains about the feet of God,

is thirty years older than the despondent cry,

> My God, thou hast forgotten me in my death.

Had the despondent view of life been the earlier and outworn creed, or had the poet, ere he closed the volume of the "Idylls of the King," already passed into that later serene faith which found expression in those faultless lyrics of his old age wherewith the arches of the Minster of the West re-echoed when his earth was laid to earth, "The Crossing of the Bar," and "The Silent Voices," then perhaps had there been throughout the "Idylls of the King" less of

> For all my mind is clouded with a doubt,

less of

> The darkness of that battle in the West,
> Where all of high and holy dies away

with which the poem closes, and there had been more of the serene faith of the poet's later years, the clear call

> Forward to the starry track
> Glimmering up the heights beyond me
> On, and always on!

more of the exultant expression of poetic faith in that aftermath of Arthurian story, "Merlin and the Gleam," that prophet-cry to the young to follow their noblest ideals, to follow the Gleam,

> O young Mariner,
> Down to the haven,
> Call your companions,
> Launch your vessel,
> And crowd your canvas,
> And, ere it vanishes
> Over the margin,
> After it, follow it,
> Follow The Gleam.

APPENDIX.

1. A Hitherto Unpublished Version of Tennyson's "To the Queen."

THE noblest men are born & bred
   Among the Saxo Norman race
   And in this world the noblest place
Madam, is yours our Queen & Head.

Your name is blown on every wind,
   Your flag thro' Austral ice is borne
   And glimmers to the Northern morn
And floats in either golden Ind.

The Poets they * that often seem
   So wretched touching mournful strings
   They likewise are a kind of kings
Nor is their empire all a dream.

Their words fly over land & main
   Their warblings make the distance glad
   Their voices heard hereafter add
A glory to a glorious reign.

A work not done by flattering state
   Nor such a lay should kings receive
   And kingly Poets should believe
The kings heart true as he is great.

---

   * There is in the MS. another *they* in this line crossed out by the pen.

APPENDIX. 153

The taskwork ode has ever fail'd :
  Not less the king in time to come
  Will seem the greater under whom
The sacred Poets have prevail'd.

I thank you that your Royal Grace
  To one of less desert allows
  This laurel greener from the brows
Of him that utter'd nothing base

I would I were as those of old
  A mellow mouth of song to fill
  Your reign with music wh might still
Be music when my lips were cold

That after men might turn the page
  And light on fancies true & sweet
  And kindle with a loyal heat
To fair Victorias golden age

But he your Laureate who succeeds
  A master such as all men quote
  Must feel as one of slender note
And piping low among the reeds.

Yet if your greatness & the care
  That yokes with splendour, yield you time
  To seek in this your Poet's rhyme
If aught of good or sweet be there

Take, Madam, this poor book of song
  For tho the faults were thick as dust
  In vacant chambers I could trust
Your kindness. May you rule us long

> And leave us scions of your blood
> As noble till the latest day.
> May children of our children say
> She wrought her people lasting good

The MS. copy of the above poem, hitherto unpublished, is in the Library of the Drexel Institute, Philadelphia. The difference between this early form of the poem, which is perhaps the first draft, and the poem as now published illustrates strikingly the poet's habit of revision. But four of the thirteen stanzas given above (and three of these in a revised form) are to be found in recent editions of the poet's works. Nine of the thirteen stanzas are now published for the first time.

This MS. copy was in the possession of the late George W. Childs. The history of the MS. will be given in a monograph describing the MSS. collected by George W. Childs and presented by him to the Library of the Drexel Institute. To the kindly interest and suggestion of the author of this forthcoming monograph, Mr. John Thomson, Librarian of the Free Library of Philadelphia, I am indebted for the knowledge of the existence of this MS.

Among the objects of interest in this collection, which will be described in the monograph, now in preparation, are an original copy of André's "Cow Chace,"* original manuscripts by Dickens, Lord Lyt-

---

* "An heroic poem in three cantos, published in London in 1781. It was originally published in Rivington's Royal Gazette, N. York, in the morning of the day on which Andre

ton, Cotton Mather, Leigh Hunt, Tom Moore, and among the most interesting two leaves of a version of Schiller's "Demetrius," differing from the same as finally published.

2. Tennyson's Punctuation and Use of Capital Letters.

The number of lines in the '57 copy, "Enid and Nimuë: The True and the False," is 2631, and there have been 431 changes in punctuation in these lines. This number would be materially increased did one compare the poem as now published, not with the '57 copy, but with the South Kensington Museum "Enid" or with the manuscript itself. There have been made also 97 minor typographical corrections to the '57 copy. This in addition to the hundreds of changes in single words * or in entire sentences.

---

was taken prisoner. The last stanza, intended to ridicule Gen. Wayne for his failure in an attempt to collect cattle for the army, is this:

'And now I've closed my epic strain;
I tremble as I show it,
Lest this same warrior-drover Wayne
Should ever catch the poet!'"

Allibone's Dictionary of Authors, J. B. Lippincott Co., Phila.

* The following verbal variations, in addition to the variations given in Chapter II., are believed to make the list complete so far as the '57 copy is concerned. Mere typographical variations are not given:

'57. Far liever had I gird his harness on him,
'73. Far lie*f*er had I gird his harness on him, (88, 22.)

From these facts it were easy to premise that which the poem "To the Queen," as above published, confirms, viz., that Lord Tennyson gave little heed to

'57. 'Thou art not worthy ev'n to speak *to* him.'
'59. 'Thou art not worthy ev'n to speak *of* him ;' (92, 23.)

'57. Indignant to the Queen; *at which* Geraint
'69. Indignant to the Queen; *whereat* Geraint (92, 26.)

'57. In a long valley, on one side *of which,*
'66. In a long valley, on one side *whereof,* (94, 16.)

'57. Far lie*v*er by his dear hand had I die
'73. Far lie*f*er by his dear hand had I die, (122, 5.)

'57. And into no Earl's *place* will I go.
'59. And into no Earl's *palace* will I go. (128, 24.)

'57. He moving homeward*s* babbled to his men
'59. He moving homeward babbled to his men, (133, 22.)

'57. In combat with the follower of *the Earl,*
'59. In combat with the follower of *Limours,* (139, 8.)

'57. '*Not so ;* not dead !' she answer'd in all haste.
'59. '*No, no,* not dead !' she answer'd in all haste. (140, 25.)

'57. *And* at the last he waken'd from his swoon,
'59. *Till* at the last he waken'd from his swoon, (142, 16.)

'57. Who love *you prince* with something of the love
'59. Who love *you, Prince,* with something of the love (150, 20.)

'57. Than if *a* knight of mine,
'59. Than if *some* knight of mine, (155, 16.)

'57. And *so* she follow'd Merlin all the way,
'59. And *then* she follow'd Merlin all the way, (190, 15.)

'57. N*o*r yet so strange as you yourself are strange,
'78. No*t* yet so strange as you yourself are strange, (194, 20.)

punctuation, the use of capital letters, and such-like
niceties of composition upon which much stress is
sometimes laid as a means toward developing the
art of authorship in the as yet mute and inglorious
Miltons of our schools.

True, there are in the '57 copy some 41 manuscript
corrections to the punctuation, but there are altogether 431 changes in punctuation, and it is hardly
probable that the poet indicated all of these upon
some other of the "six trial copies printed."

K. It buzzes *wildly* round the point;
'73. It buzzes *fiercely* round the point; (199, 13.)

'57. Were proving it *upon* me, and that I lay
'59. Were proving it *on* me, and that I lay (199, 17.)

'57. *True:* Love, tho' Love were of the grossest,
'73. *Yea!* Love, tho' Love were of the grossest, (200, 16.)

'57. So lean, his eyes were monstrous, *but* the skin
'59. So lean his eyes were monstrous; *while* the skin (206, 24.)

'57. *But* since he kept his mind on one sole aim,
'59. *And* since he kept his mind on one sole aim, (207, 1.)

'57. And darkling felt the sculptured ornament*
'59. And darkling felt the sculptured ornament (211, 9.)

'57. And *want* the will to lift their eyes and see
'59. *Without* the will to lift their eyes, and see (215, 11.)

'57. *And* while she sat,
'59. *There* while she sat, (218, 2.)

'57. Who knows, once more. *O*, what was once
'75. Who knows? once more. *Lo!* what was once (218, 21.)

K. Farewell,—think *kindly* of me,
'59. Farewell; think *gently* of me, (218, 24.)

It is manifest from the changes made since the publication of the '57 copy (no less than from the MS. above published) that the poet followed no consistent rule for the use of capital letters. Indeed there is in his poems no consistent use of capitals in any edition. We find in the same poem queen and Queen, earl and Earl, prince and Prince, heaven and Heaven, king and King. In the '57 copy, though we find the Queen, the Earl, etc., we have uniformly, except on two pages (at the beginning of "Nimuë") king with a small *k*. Apparently another compositor began to "set up" "Nimuë," and after two pages were in type he was called from the work or directed to change to a small *k* in the case of the word king. On these two pages where we find the King in '57 we find also Bard, Wizard, Seer, which elsewhere in the '57 copy are bard, wizard, seer.

In the '59 edition we find for some 87 pages king, then King until within 10 pages of the close, where we have king again. The change from King to king is made in the middle of page 134.

The '69 edition follows the '59 uniformly in this respect. In '73 we have in every case the King, even when the King is not King Arthur. In '92 we have "a petty king," "his brother king," "the kings," "this king," "a King." "the Cornish king," "the holy king," but always "the King." We have "this last, dim, weird battle of the west," and "a bitter wind, clear from the North," "they came. . . . toward the sunrise," and "we have heard from our wise men at home to Northward." Manifestly, the variations in the use of capital letters preclude any possibility of finding a rule for their use.

3. Is there another '57 Copy in Existence?

In a review of the "Idylls of the King" in the *North British Review* (August, 1859) occurs a line, presumably quoted from the poem, "Snatching his great limbs from the bed." But this form of the line is not quoted from the first ('59) edition of the "Idylls of the King" which the reviewer was discussing, but is a reminiscence of the '57 copy. In the '59 edition the line is,

At this he hurl'd his huge limbs out of bed,

In the '57 copy we find, not exactly "Snatching his great limbs from the bed," but

At this he snatched his great limbs from the bed,

How did the line from the '57 unpublished copy get into a review of the first published edition? Manifestly, in case the reviewer quoted only the lines which are exactly alike in the '57 copy and the '59 edition no inferences are possible. But if he quoted some of the lines which differ in the '57 copy and the '59 edition, and quoted them as they are given in the '57 copy, then some inference may properly be drawn as to the text which he had before him as he wrote.

In general the quotations from the poem as given in the review agree with the '59 edition, even in the cases in which the '59 edition differs from the '57 copy. There are, however, the following striking similarities with the '57 copy:

'57. At this he snatched his great limbs from the bed,
Rev.   Snatching his great limbs from the bed,
'59. At this he hurl'd his huge limbs out of bed,

'57. In combat with the follower of the Earl,
Rev. In combat with the follower of the earl,
'59. In combat with the follower of Limours,

'57. At Merlin's feet the wileful Nimuë lay.
Rev. At Merlin's feet the wilful Vivien lay.
'59. At Merlin's feet the wily Vivien lay.

It is patent that the writer of the review had read the '57 version of "Enid and Nimuë," even if he had not one of the "six trial-copies printed" before him as he wrote. On being shown the similarities above quoted, Dr. Richard Garnett, Keeper of Printed Books of the British Museum, and also one of his assistants, independently suggested the poet Coventry Patmore as being in all probability the writer of the review; or, if not he, then Lord Houghton. Both of these authors were intimate friends of Tennyson, and both were at that time frequent contributors to the *North British Review*.

The belief of the makers of the catalogue in the Library of the British Museum that "This copy, bearing Lord Tennyson's autograph inscription," is "the sole survivor of six trial-copies printed" is based, we must assume, upon good grounds. Yet if

APPENDIX.

it is not more than "believed," if it is not positively *known*, that the remaining five trial-copies have been destroyed, it is possible that another copy, showing some of the many corrections adopted in the '59 edition but not contained in the British Museum copy, and showing also, perhaps, many tentative revisions not adopted, may yet be found in the library of either Mr. Coventry Patmore or Lord Houghton.

THE END.

www.ingramcontent.com/pod-product-compliance
Lightning Source LLC
Chambersburg PA
CBHW031457160426
43195CB00010BB/1013